Pelican Books

# The Law Machine

Marcel Berlins, a former practising lawyer and civil servant, was a leader writer and legal correspondent of *The Times* until 1982. Now a freelance writer, he is the author of several books on legal themes and has presented a number of television series, including 'The Law Machine'.

Clare Dyer is a solicitor, formerly on the staff of the Law Society. She writes on legal topics for a number of newspapers and magazines. Together with Marcel Berlins, she is the author of *Living Together* (1982).

# The Law Machine

Marcel Berlins and Clare Dyer

Penguin Books

Penguin Books Ltd, Harmondsworth, Middlesex, England
Viking Penguin Inc., 40 West 23rd Street, New York, New York 10010, U.S.A.
Penguin Books Australia Ltd, Ringwood, Victoria, Australia
Penguin Books Canada Limited, 2801 John Street, Markham, Ontario, Canada L3R 1B4
Penguin Books (N.Z.) Ltd, 182–190 Wairau Road, Auckland 10, New Zealand

First published 1982
Second edition 1986

Made and printed in Great Britain by Cox & Wyman Ltd, Reading
Set in AM Varityper Bembo

# Contents

# Introduction

The aim of this book is to explain, we hope clearly and entertainingly, how the machinery of justice – the law machine – actually works in practice. It is not designed to probe the content of particular laws, or to provide a guide to your rights. But laws and rights can only be properly understood if there is an appreciation of the legal process of which they form part. A law on its own is meaningless unless it can be channelled through an effective legal machinery.

The book arose originally from a London Weekend Television series 'The Law Machine', which was transmitted in 1983. For the first time on British television lawyers – barristers and solicitors – and judges appeared not just as interviewees or panelists, but doing their normal job. The series took as its starting point a fictitious motor accident in which a car driven by John Smith ran into a pedestrian, Anne Jones. It followed Smith through to his appearance at the Crown Court, where he was prosecuted for reckless driving, and then looked at Anne Jones' attempt to get compensation for her injuries in the High Court. The two trials on which the series focused were the most realistic ever staged on British television. Smith and Jones and the witnesses were played by actors, but the lawyers were practising barristers and solicitors treating the trial, and the conferences and negotiations leading up to it, just as they would have done in a real case. The judges were highly experienced, recently retired judges. The jury was chosen in the same way as a real jury. No part of the trial – including the jury's verdict and the High Court judge's decision – was scripted. Nor were any of the meetings between the lawyers and their clients.

The book uses the staged trials as a useful device for explaining the way the criminal and the civil processes work. We have also quoted from interviews which appeared in the series, and some which had to be excluded from the final version. Where there is no specific citation for a quotation, it has been taken, with permission of London Weekend Television, from the television programmes. The book, however, deals with far more than the series was able to do in the relatively short time available. Many aspects of the machinery of justice which had to be omitted altogether, or were only touched on in the programmes, are described in detail here.

In preparing this second edition, we were greatly helped by those kind enough to read sections of the book and offer their valuable comments: Walter Merricks, Jenny Turner, James Morton, Rodger Pannone, Gerry Moggridge, Derek Howard, Simon Hillyard, Allen Davies and Rosanna Del Maestro. Barbara Ellis was a meticulous and understanding editor.

To avoid awkwardness and the constant repetition of 'he or she' and 'his or her', we have used the male pronoun to include the female. The system we describe is that of England and Wales – Scotland and Northern Ireland have their own.

Marcel Berlins

Clare Dyer

May 1986

# CHAPTER I

# JUSTICE FOR ALL?

In an average year Parliament passes between seventy and one hundred new acts, some just a page or two, others running to over a hundred pages. Every year ministers and Government departments make over 2,000 new sets of rules and regulations, which also have the full force of law. In hundreds of court cases every year, judges interpret, restate and redefine the law. In the process, new rights are created and new obligations and restrictions are imposed.

The ordinary citizen has only the vaguest notion of what the law expects of him and what it can do for him. Not only is he largely ignorant of the legal remedies open to him, he is likely to be at a loss to know where to take his legal problem – or even to identify it as a problem with a legal solution.

The English legal system has many shortcomings. Yet even an entirely fault-free system must be counted a failure if it doesn't reach a large proportion of those who need it. Access is the first weak point in the law machine.

## Access to the law

Where do people take their legal problems? It depends. Certain types of problem are identified in the public mind with solicitors. Well over 90 per cent of house-buyers, for instance, consult solicitors. Criminal charges and divorce are also normally seen as matters needing legal help and advice. So are making a will and dealing with the estate of someone who has died. But many essentially legal problems rarely come to solicitors: whether or not someone qualifies for a social security benefit, for example, and what to do if benefit is refused. The problem – if it is seen as capable of a solution at all – will not be seen as a legal one.

Even someone whose problem is more obviously a legal one – for example, a tenant threatened with eviction – is liable to be put off seeing a solicitor by fear of the cost, and by not knowing the form. In court cases between landlords and tenants, most landlords have lawyers representing them; tenants rarely do.

The 900 Citizens' Advice Bureaux in England and Wales are an

9

invaluable filter into the legal system, simply because they tackle all sorts of problems. Therefore, as long as someone recognizes he has a problem, he need not diagnose it himself as a legal one. The advice worker analyses the problem and refers it to the appropriate place for treatment – if possible not just to any solicitor but to a solicitor known to be experienced in the particular type of work. Over half the inquiries which come to CABx have some legal content. The advice workers can deal with some of the queries: explaining legislation, filling in forms, making telephone calls, drafting letters or referring the inquirer to a specialist agency. A few CABx have their own salaried lawyers on tap, but most bureaux refer their more difficult legal queries to local solicitors.

Bringing the solicitor to the client can help overcome the reluctance felt by many people to enter the unfamiliar territory of a solicitor's office. Nearly half the CABx in England and Wales have visiting lawyers in attendance, usually once a week. Consultations are free, but if the case requires action, the solicitor can take the inquirer on as a client, or refer him to another solicitor. Then he either applies for legal aid or becomes a fee-paying client, depending on his means.

But many people who could be helped by the law are unaware of the services offered by the CAB. Others go unhelped simply because it never occurs to them that any help might be available to them. Accident victims are the most obvious example.

Not every accident victim has a legal remedy. Some accidents are nobody's fault. But the law allows anyone injured by someone else's negligence to claim compensation for his financial loss and his pain and suffering. Most serious accidents are someone else's fault – usually traffic accidents and accidents at work. The fact that the victim may be partly responsible – by not wearing his seat-belt, or his protective clothing at work – does not prevent him from claiming compensation. It simply reduces the amount of money he gets. But studies have shown that surprisingly few accident victims, even with quite serious injuries, realize they can claim compensation. A recent study done by the Centre for Socio-Legal Studies at Oxford found that only one in four seriously injured accident victims even thought about claiming damages. And of those who considered the possibility, only just over half actually took legal advice. Fewer than one in eight got compensation through going to law.

How can the legal system even begin to help those who are simply unaware that it has anything to offer them? A scheme designed to improve access to the law for accident victims, which started in Manchester, has thrown up findings which could usefully be applied nationally and extended to other areas of the law. In 1979 the Greater Manchester Legal Services Committee set up a scheme to help accident victims exercise their rights. The committee had three tasks: to make accident victims realize they might have a claim, to overcome their uncertainty about how to approach a solicitor, and to allay their fears about possible costs. Leaflets and posters are sent out to hospitals, doctors' surgeries, CABx, libraries, DHSS offices and advice agencies. The leaflet offers a free interview with a solicitor. All the accident victim has to do is fill in his name and address and send the coupon off. The solicitor assigned to his case gets in touch and suggests an appointment.

Research done on the first twenty-one months of operation indicated that a scheme like this, operated nationally, would probably recover well over £1m a year in compensation for accident victims who would otherwise get nothing. In its first twenty-one months the Manchester scheme collected a total of £136,742, including one settlement of £30,000 for a man with irreversible brain damage, whose wife had abandoned the claim two years earlier when she was turned down for legal aid. Of the Manchester claimants 42 per cent said the idea of claiming compensation had not occurred to them before they saw the leaflet. Two-thirds had never been to a solicitor in their lives and many admitted that they would never have taken the step on their own initiative.

By early 1986, one in four local law societies were running accident schemes. Publicity of the sort given to these schemes, available at the point where those who need it would be likely to see it, is the only effective way of getting over the first big hurdle blocking access to the legal system – the lack of awareness of what the system has to offer.

## Cost

Fear of the cost is the second deterrent to seeking legal help. Newspapers regularly carry frightening stories about losers in legal actions who face bills of tens of thousands of pounds. These scare stories put off even those in the lowest income group, whose lawyers' fees would be covered entirely by legal aid. About 60 per cent of the population qualify for free or cheap help under the legal aid scheme, which pays lawyers in private practice from government funds for looking after the legal needs of the less well-off. Many of the accident victims in the Manchester scheme got legal aid to pursue their claims. But Hazel Genn of the Centre for Socio-Legal Studies comments in her research report on the scheme: 'Fear of the expense involved in seeking legal advice was . . . pervasive . . . The extent to which the accident victims were ignorant of the Legal Aid and Legal Advice schemes is disconcerting.'

Legal aid is discussed in detail in Chapter IX. It is touched on here because access to justice can often hinge on the granting or withholding of legal aid. The legal aid scheme has put the law and its remedies within the reach of the little man. But the middle classes – except for divorcing wives – are largely ineligible, while still unable to afford what Lord Devlin, a former law lord, has described as our

'Rolls Royce' legal system. The Royal Commission on Legal Services recommended in 1979 that everyone should be entitled to legal aid, with the better-off paying substantial contributions. But with the cost of legal aid soaring, this recommendation is a non-starter and the percentage of people eligible for legal aid is likely to drop.

Legal aid also has its gaps. More and more decisions which affect the lives of ordinary people are made not by courts, but by tribunals. An industrial tribunal decides whether someone has been unfairly dismissed from his job. National insurance tribunals and supplementary benefit appeal tribunals decide whether someone should get a welfare benefit, if DHSS officers have turned him down. But legal aid is still not available for representation by a lawyer before most tribunals.

Applicants for legal aid in a civil case have to satisfy two tests. They have to be within the financial limits, and they must have a reasonable case. But the chances of getting legal aid can depend on where you live. In the North, over 14 per cent of applicants are turned down, against only 4 per cent in South Wales, a situation the Lord Chancellor's permanent secretary has admitted is 'manifestly unsatisfactory'.

Legal aid is also available for representation by a lawyer in criminal cases. In the Crown Court, where the more serious charges are tried, legal aid is freely given. Around 95 per cent of the defendants have their defences paid for by the state. Legal aid is usually granted as long as the financial test is satisfied – broadly, if the defendant needs help in meeting the cost of his defence – which it almost always is, since few defendants can afford to finance the costs of a Crown Court trial out of their own pockets.

In the magistrates' court, however, where the less serious 98 per cent of criminal cases are disposed of, legal aid is more discretionary. Some courts are more liberal than others. Yet for many defendants, no legal aid means no lawyer. A survey by the Widgery Committee on Legal Aid in Criminal Proceedings in 1964 found that only one-third of defendants turned down for legal aid on the grounds that they could afford to pay actually retained a lawyer when they came to court. But a small study done in 1972 by Professor Michael Zander of the London School of Economics found that representation by a lawyer more than doubled the chances of acquittal.

## Duty solicitors

One development of the 1970s which has meant a greater access to justice in the magistrates' court is the duty solicitor scheme. Over 300 courts are covered by duty solicitors, who are on call to advise defendants. Should a defendant plead guilty or is there a defence worth pursuing? If the plea is to be 'not guilty', the solicitor can apply for bail and ask for an adjournment to allow time to apply for legal aid and prepare the case. A study of duty solicitor schemes done by Michael King for the Cobden Trust in 1976 found that significantly more defendants represented by duty solicitors got bail and legal aid than those who were unrepresented. If the defendant pleads guilty, the duty solicitor can make a 'plea in mitigation', putting forward reasons which might influence the magistrates to impose a lighter sentence than they might otherwise.

Duty solicitor schemes are in operation in over half the magistrates' courts in the country, including most of the busier courts. Legal aid pays for the duty solicitor's advice and help. Since 1 January 1986, when the Police and Criminal Evidence Act 1984 gave suspects the right of access to legal advice in the police station, duty solicitors have been available on a twenty-four-hour basis to attend police stations. Advice, which is free to the suspect, is paid for by legal aid. In the past, studies have shown as few as 2 per cent of suspects in the police station were allowed access to a solicitor. In a few county courts, law centre workers or CAB workers act as duty solicitors, mostly for small debtors and tenants faced with eviction by local councils and private landlords.

## Finding the right solicitor

How does someone who has – or thinks he has – a legal problem find the right solicitor to handle it? The system is extraordinarily hit and miss, and very little has so far been done in this country to achieve the right match between solicitor and client.

Several studies have investigated how people actually find a solicitor. In one involving two samples of divorcing parents, done by Mervyn Murch of Bristol University, by far the most popular method of choosing was through the recommendation of family or friends. The next largest group went to a solicitor they had used before – in many cases for their house purchase. Nearly one person in six had simply noticed a solicitor's office and walked in, or chosen a firm from the yellow pages. Only about one in eight asked the CAB or a social worker, though in most areas the CAB will be the agency with most experience of local solicitors and their work.

The Royal Commission on Legal Services surveyed a representative sample of people who consulted a solicitor for the first time in 1977. The findings were similar:

> Most people going to a particular lawyer for the first time were led to him through their personal or informal contacts – through the recommendation or experience of their relatives, friends, neighbours or workmates. It was only in a quarter of cases of first consultation in 1977 that the client found a lawyer through recommendation or mention by an official body or by someone else with whom he already had business or professional dealings.

The Royal Commission on Legal Services 1979 urged that solicitors should be allowed to advertise, for example, their fees and 'recognized specialisms'. This presupposes a machinery for recognizing specialization which hardly exists in this country at the moment. In some states of America, lawyers who have taken extra exams or handled a certain number of cases in a particular area of law can be described as specialists in directories and can advertise themselves as such. Here, the prospective client has no way of locating a specialist solicitor – though many exist – other than by haphazard word of mouth.

The Royal Commission proposed a simple system which would allow solicitors to be recognized as specialists in one or two subjects, and to advertise the fact. They suggested that the Law Society could vet applications from solicitors who had practised in a particular field of law for at least two years, spending at least a quarter of their time each year working in that field.

The society keeps panels of solicitors who are considered competent and experienced in two specialized fields: child care law and mental health law. The Civil Justice Review, set up by the Lord Chancellor to suggest reforms to improve the machinery of civil justice, has proposed allowing only specialist solicitors to handle personal injury cases, and the Law Society is considering setting up a panel for this sort of work. The Lay Observer, an official who monitors the Law Society's handling of complaints against solicitors, has pinpointed the readiness of solicitors to take on work – particularly personal injury cases – at which they are not sufficiently expert as a cause of client dissatisfaction.

Since 1985, solicitors have been allowed to advertise the type of work they do and the fees they charge. They are still not allowed, however, to claim any particular expertise or specialization. The new freedom to advertise has not changed the way in which people find their solicitors. In a survey carried out for the Law Society in early 1986, 60 per cent of people sampled chose a solicitor through the personal recommendation of friends, relatives, colleagues or other professionals, and only 2 per cent through seeing an advertisement.

The Law Society – the solicitors' professional body – prefers not to recommend one solicitor over another. The *Solicitors' Regional Directory*, published by the society, lists all solicitors with details of the sorts of work each solicitor undertakes. Solicitors are asked to assign numbers to the different types of work they do, to show which category – for example, conveyancing or family law – occupies most of their time, which the next biggest chunk, and so on. But the information is not vetted, and some of it may be inaccurate.

## Other sources of help

For many people the prospect of visiting a solicitor's office can be rather forbidding. Law centres, with their shop-front offices and casually dressed staff, seem more approachable. For those fortunate enough to receive it, law centre help is usually of quite a high standard. The trouble is that law centres are thin on the ground. There are only about fifty in England and Wales, all but one in big cities. Run by salaried lawyers and advice workers, these offer a free legal service to the poorer section of the community in their catchment area, although there is no formal means test. So as not to compete with solicitors in private practice, they are not allowed to do certain types of work – divorce, conveyancing, and large personal injury cases, for example – and they tend to concentrate on housing, employment, juvenile crime and child care cases. Law centres have good contacts with private solicitors in their area, particularly those who do law-centre-type work, and will refer clients to outside solicitors if they cannot take on a job themselves. Some law centres prefer to spread their resources by concentrating on groups, rather than individuals – for example, tackling a local authority over disrepair on a whole council estate.

In some areas legal advice centres – run by local authorities, church groups, residents' associations or other agencies – offer free advice but (unlike law centres) won't take on cases and see them through. These centres usually have no legally qualified staff of their own, but depend on volunteer lawyers who are willing to give up some of their spare time.

Most trade unions offer legal help and advice to their members. Some offer general advice; others restrict themselves to legal problems connected with the member's job – such as accidents at work, sacking, breaches of the employment contract. Some unions have their own legal departments which handle negotiations in accident cases, and represent union members at industrial tribunals. Unions also retain solicitors in private practice to deal with accident claims on behalf of their members.

Many other organizations provide legal help or simple advice to members or to the general public, on either a commercial or a voluntary basis. The Automobile Association, for example, has its own legal staff which deals with members' motoring-related legal problems. MIND (The National Association for Mental Health) and the Child Poverty Action Group are two examples of voluntary agencies who will advise, take up cases and provide representation before tribunals. Some local authorities run housing and consumer advice centres, and government-funded bodies like the Equal Opportunities Commission and the Commission for Racial Equality will answer legal queries in their own fields and help with tribunals and court cases

## Do-it-yourself law

Given the gaps in legal aid – rarely given for consumer claims under
£500 – and the cost of legal services (which we explore in more detail
in Chapter IX), what scope is there for taking the law into your own
hands?

Britain is a nation of do-it-yourselfers. If you can do your own
gardening, car maintenance and decorating, why not a DIY will,
conveyance or divorce? Will-making is superficially simple, and
home-made wills are common, but many of them turn out to be
invalid, usually because of the simplest mistakes, like failing to sign
the will or have it properly witnessed. DIY conveyancing is still
fairly uncommon because the legal procedure for buying and selling
houses is complicated and time-consuming, and full of unfamiliar
jargon. And most people are unwilling to take a chance that
something might go wrong when such large sums are involved. But
step-by-step manuals are available for DIY lawyers who are
prepared to tackle conveyancing, will-making, divorce-by-post, and
the work involved in sorting out an estate.

## Small claims

Attempts have been made to cut through the courts' red tape and
allow more ordinary individuals to operate the system themselves.
Two small claims courts set up experimentally in the 1970s, in
Manchester and London, allowed consumer claims – for instance
over a pair of shoes that split after only a few days wear – to be
settled easily, quickly and cheaply. Provided both parties agreed,
claims were settled by arbitration rather than a court hearing. The
arbitrator, usually a lawyer but sometimes an expert in the
particular trade involved – for example, an automotive engineer if
the argument was over a faulty secondhand car – would get round a
table with the two parties, hear both sides, ask questions, and make a
decision in favour of one or the other. Representation by lawyers
was banned. Unfortunately, funds ran out and both these schemes
had to close.

The county courts, set up in the middle of the last century, were
meant to provide the little man with quick, cheap justice. The
procedure was supposed to be simple enough to allow people to
pursue their claims without lawyers. But the rules of procedure for
the county court now fill 2,000 pages. In the 1970s a small claims
procedure was set up within the county court, with registrars (senior
court officials, formerly practising solicitors) acting as arbitrators.
Lawyers are not banned, but in most cases the loser won't be ordered
to pay the winner's costs. So the consumer risks only the court fees if
he loses.

All claims up to £500 now go automatically to arbitration though a trial may be allowed in certain cases. Rules introduced in 1981 encourage registrars to help the DIY litigant by taking a more Active role in the arbitration. CAB workers are trained to help with bringing a case to court and court officials are encouraged to explain procedure and help with filling in forms.

But the small claims procedure is still not the quick, cheap, do-it-yourself method it was designed to be. Cases going to arbitration take just as long to come to a conclusion as other cases, just as many firms as individuals use the small claims procedure, and in many cases at least one side – usually a company or shopkeeper – is represented by a lawyer.

Having gone through what is still for many people a daunting and protracted procedure and won the case, the successful litigant is all too often let down by the ineffective system for enforcing judgments. However, the small claims procedure is now on the agenda for reform, as part of the Civil Justice Review.

# CHAPTER II

# THE COURTS

The courtroom is the pivot of the English system of justice. For centuries it has been the setting for the final settlement of disputes, whether between the state and one of its citizens said to have committed a wrong against society, or between individuals. And because the contest in court can be so crucial to the disputants – much more than in most other countries, where many of the more important decisions are taken before trial – the English courtroom has been invested with a sense of high drama and tension. Lives can be ruined there and fortunes made. What God has joined together can, in a court, be put asunder. One judge, three magistrates or twelve ordinary men and women can hold in their hands a person's freedom, reputation, wealth, home, marriage and happiness.

Richard Ingrams, editor of the satirical magazine *Private Eye*, a frequent participant in court battles, looks on the law court as a casino: 'When a judge begins to sum up, it's like someone has turned a roulette and we look anxiously to see if the ball has fallen in the black or the red.' The American journalist H. L. Mencken described a courtroom as a place where Jesus Christ and Judas Iscariot would be equals, with the betting odds in favour of Judas. Books and television programmes have confirmed the courtroom as a place of drama and uncertainty, where justice fights injustice and often lands up on the losing side, and where victory depends on fate, often in the guise of a last-minute surprise witness.

The reality is very different. The activities of an English court are, for the most part, of little interest to anyone other than the parties involved. Far from crackling with electric tension, the atmosphere droops with soporific indifference. Every now and again there is a criminal trial which excites public interest because of the personality involved – like Jeremy Thorpe, former Liberal Party leader and one of Britain's best-known politicians, charged with conspiracy to murder in 1978 – or the magnitude of the crime – the Yorkshire Ripper, the Great Train Robbery – or the issues raised – Dr Leonard Arthur and the death of a severely handicapped baby under his care, the *Gay News* poem linking Christ and homosexuality, or Clive Ponting and his leaking of background information on the Falklands War. But the vast majority of criminal trials are humdrum affairs. Indeed, most defendants plead guilty and all that is done in the courtroom is the sentencing. Whether or not he goes to prison, and for how long, is of course tremendously important to the defendant and to those close to him. But it is not often the stuff of great drama, and much else that happens in court is merely formal or procedural: commitals for trial, remands, requests for bail.

The civil courts present an even drier prospect to the outside observer. Here too there is much that is mere conveyor-belt procedure: various kinds of applications and petitions to the court which do not involve a real contest. In trials which are fought out, argument on legal points often takes up a large part of the time, and even the cross-examination of witnesses seldom raises the low-key pitch of the proceedings. The Court of Appeal very rarely hears witnesses at all, and the appeal is based mainly or totally on legal argument, impenetrable to those who are uninitiated in the jargon.

The visual image that most people have of an English court is becoming increasingly wrong, too. Those elegant, high-ceilinged, wood-panelled rooms, with the judge viewing proceedings from his vantage point behind a resplendent oak table on a raised platform, are dying out. The new courts are small, functional, low-ceilinged, often lit with artificial fluorescent lighting. The judge's pedestal has shrunk and he is nearer and lower. The effect is bland, clinical and cheerless.

## THE STRUCTURE OF THE COURTS

Like so many other English legal institutions, the court system defies logical analysis. It is the product of 900 years of development, much of it haphazard and unplanned, punctuated by occasional attempts by Parliament to bring some order into it and adapt it to changing needs. There is certainly a recognizable hierarchy, with the House of Lords as the 'highest court in the land' (though its supremacy is now questionable, since accession to the European Community made our laws subject to the European Court in Luxembourg). But it is not a straightforward, clearly mapped out pyramid structure, as in most other countries. There are deviations and quirks and historical accidents clouding the symmetry. Probably the most logical dividing line is between the criminal and the civil courts, though in fact some courts do both kinds of work.

What is the difference between civil and criminal cases? In a criminal case someone is *prosecuted* for behaviour which is considered harmful to society as a whole – a crime, like murder or burglary. Normally the prosecution is brought by the state (usually in the shape of the police), but individuals can prosecute too. If found guilty, the offender will be punished by the state.

Civil cases are between private interests. One individual – or possibly a firm, a local authority or some other body – *sues* another, usually for some harm caused to him personally, or for money owed to him. Perhaps the person he is suing has run him down and fractured his leg or has broken a contract. The police will not be interested unless – as sometimes happens – the same behaviour also amounts to a crime. For example, a driver who knocks down a pedestrian may be guilty of the crime of reckless driving. The same accident gives the victim the right to sue the driver for the tort (legal jargon for a civil wrong) of negligence. So the driver can be prosecuted for reckless driving in a criminal court, convicted and sent to prison or ordered to pay a fine, which goes to the state. Later he may be sued by the person he has injured, found negligent, and be ordered to pay compensation to the victim for the injury suffered. Or he may win one case and lose the other, because different things have to be proved in civil and criminal cases. The degree of proof required is also different. In criminal cases there can only be a conviction if the case has been proved 'beyond reasonable doubt' – very near certainty. A civil case is won on a 'balance of probabilities' – more likely than not.

In civil cases, the person suing is known as the plaintiff, and the person sued is called the defendant. In criminal cases, the person accused of the crime may be called either the accused or the defendant.

The distinction between a crime and a civil wrong was highlighted recently when an intruder broke into the Queen's bedroom. Entering someone else's home without permission is trespass: not a crime, but a civil wrong. It only becomes a crime if the intruder uses violence, or causes damage – by breaking a lock or a window, for example – or if he intends to commit a crime (such as theft) once inside. Because Michael Fagan's intrusion was a simple trespass, he could not be prosecuted. But a trespasser can be sued in the civil courts.

New crimes are being created all the time, as society revises its thinking about the sorts of behaviour it wants to discourage. For example, not wearing a car seat belt is a new criminal offence for drivers and front seat passengers. After the Queen's ordeal there were calls by MPs for trespass to be made a crime.

Originally courts derived their jurisdiction from the reigning monarch. They were in theory the Queen's courts. Many of them were literally the courts of the sovereign, directly responsible to him or her. But it is now a cherished and indispensable aspect of all our courts that they must be independent of the monarch. It is another fundamental principle of English justice that what happens in the courts should be open and public. There are exceptions, such as where young children are involved, or there is a risk to national security. But in general English justice is open justice, and any member of the public can see what goes on in any court.

This section gives an outline of the structure and jurisdiction of the courts themselves: the judges, magistrates and other personnel of the courts are discussed more fully in chapters III-V.

# Magistrates' courts

Magistrates' courts are the people's courts, formerly popularly known as police courts, the lowest tier in the criminal justice system. They have been with us in one form or another for 600 years, and magistrates (justices of the peace, or JPs) for even longer. Originally a sort of primitive policing agency, justices of the peace were given their judicial role in the fourteenth century. The magistrates and their courts have undergone a number of changes in their status, jurisdiction and reputation since then but the fundamental basis of their existence has remained the same. Justice is delivered not by professional judges or lawyers, but by appointed representatives of the community.

The system of unpaid, lay, part-time magistrates is unique in the world. There are more than 27,000 lay magistrates (plus sixty paid, legally qualified magistrates), sitting in the 700 or so courts in England and Wales (the system is different in Scotland and Northern Ireland). They deal with three million cases a year – 98 per cent of all criminal cases – and perform a variety of other functions as well.

Their main job is to deliver 'summary justice' to people charged with less serious crimes. (Grave offences are dealt with at the Crown Court). But the fact that they deal with the lower end of the criminal market does not mean that the punishments they impose are necessarily trivial. For some offences magistrates can send offenders to prison for six months.

Most defendants who come before the magistrates' courts plead guilty to the charges against them and all the magistrates need to do is to pass sentence on them, or, occasionally, to send them to the Crown Court for a stiffer punishment than the magistrates have the power to impose. For those who plead not guilty, there may be a choice between having their trial by magistrates but no jury, or going to the Crown Court for a jury trial. For most offences, however, there is no choice – the law lays down whether the charge is to be heard by the magistrates or in the Crown Court.

Trial and sentencing are not the only functions of magistrates' courts in the criminal justice system. Magistrates make crucial decisions over whether to grant a defendant bail or to remand him to prison to wait for his trial. They act, too, as filters through which more serious criminal cases pass. Almost all criminal prosecutions which reach the Crown Court are committed there by the magistrates' court.

Usually a committal involves simply putting written statements before the court, without the need for witnesses to tell their stories in court. Occasionally, though, a defendant exercises his right to test the evidence against him by having prosecution witnesses give evidence, and cross-examining them. The magistrates then have to

# CIVIL

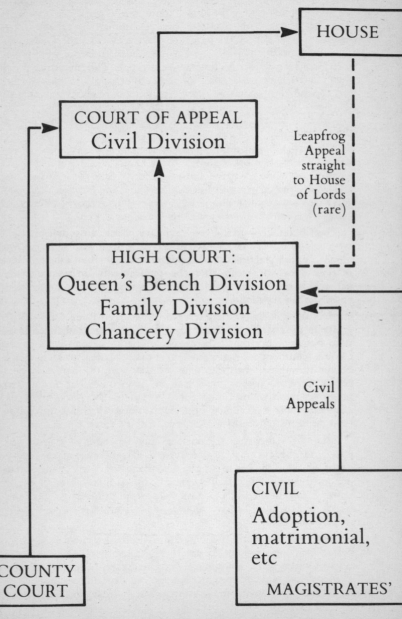

HOUSE

COURT OF APPEAL
Civil Division

Leapfrog
Appeal
straight
to House
of Lords
(rare)

HIGH COURT:
Queen's Bench Division
Family Division
Chancery Division

Civil
Appeals

CIVIL
Adoption,
matrimonial,
etc

MAGISTRATES'

COUNTY
COURT

# CRIMINAL

OF LORDS

COURT OF APPEAL
Criminal Division

CROWN COURT

Criminal appeals
on point of
law only to
Queen's Bench
Divisional Court.
Then to
House of Lords

Criminal
Appeals

CRIMINAL

COURT

Simplified diagram of English courts

decide whether the case made out against him is enough to justify committal to the Crown Court. Jeremy Thorpe, for instance, exercised that right when faced with a charge of conspiracy to murder. The magistrates at Minehead in Somerset committed him for trial to the Old Bailey, where he was acquitted.

Children under seventeen accused of criminal offences are usually dealt with in juvenile courts. They are supposed to be more informal and less frightening than the adult courts, and separated from them. Juvenile courts stress the care and treatment of young delinquents, rather than their punishment. Because they deal with such sensitive matters, the public is excluded from these courts. The magistrates who sit in juvenile courts are specially selected from the pool of all justices for their knowledge of and interest in children.

They can order child offenders to serve time in an attendance centre (for a specified number of hours, often on a Saturday afternoon), or (boys only) to go to a detention centre, for between three weeks and four months. If the child is 15 or over he can be given a youth custody order. Juvenile magistrates can also fine young offenders, and if they have no money their parents can be ordered to pay the fine. Magistrates also have the crucial power to place a child in the care of the local authority. This is not limited to delinquents: magistrates can make a care order whenever they believe that a child is being neglected or harmed by a parent or is beyond parental control.

Magistrates have a rag-bag of other responsibilities. They have a wide jurisdiction in family matters. For instance, they can grant maintenance to a separated wife or husband, or for a child; they can make affiliation orders, confirming the paternity of an illegitimate child and ordering the father to pay maintenance; they can order a violent spouse out of the home to protect the other partner or any children.

The courts are also responsible for granting drink licences to pubs and restaurants, and licences for betting shops and casinos. It is a duty which justices take seriously. They are no rubber stamp, as the Ladbroke and Playboy casino empires discovered to their cost; their activities came to a stop as a direct result of the refusal of five licensing magistrates to renew their licences.

Requests for extradition – where a foreign state asks for the return of a wanted alleged criminal living in Britain – are heard at the Bow Street magistrates' court, by a stipendary magistrate.

## Crown Courts

Crown courts have existed only since 1972, when they replaced the ancient quarter sessions and assize courts. They are the places where all the serious crimes are tried, such as murder, rape, arson, armed robbery, fraud and so on, as well as some less serious offences. For example, even the most trivial theft, involving only a few pence, can be dealt with in the Crown Court if the accused wants it. And if the accused pleads not guilty to the charge, then he or she has the ancient and time-honoured right to trial by jury. When there is a jury, the judge's role is limited to deciding matters of law and summing-up to the jury. The jury decides whether the defendant is guilty or not guilty. But of around 100,000 defendants dealt with by the Crown Court in 1984, only about 30,000 had trials by jury. The others pleaded guilty and only needed to be sentenced.

There are about ninety Crown Court centres in England and Wales, many of them consisting of several courtrooms. According to the seriousness of the charges, cases can be tried by High Court judges (the most important crimes – murder, for instance – or particularly sensitive cases), circuit judges (who hear the majority of Crown Court trials), or part-time recorders.

The most famous Crown Court in England, perhaps the most famous court in the world, is the Old Bailey, or more properly, the Central Criminal Court. Built on the site of the notorious Newgate Prison, the Old Bailey has been host to some of the most famous and infamous murderers in English history – among them Crippen, Christie, the Yorkshire Ripper, the Kray twins, and Ruth Ellis, the last woman to be hanged for murder in England. For many of them it was their last public appearance before the gallows. Oscar Wilde and William Joyce, wartime's Lord Haw-Haw, were among other participants in the court's dramatic history.

The death penalty has now been abolished; crowds seldom queue for hours to get into an Old Bailey court as they used to. And the great barristers of the Court's golden era, Edward Marshall Hall, Patrick Hastings and Norman Birkett, have been replaced by humdrum, less flamboyant, less eccentric barristers, boring perhaps but effective. Most of the Old Bailey's nineteen courts are now in a new uninspiring annexe, lacking all atmosphere. But the figure on the dome of the building of the lady holding the scales of justice (and, contrary to public belief, not blindfolded) remains one of the enduring symbols of justice in a free society.

The Crown Court acts also as the appeal court against both convictions and sentences by magistrates. When the appeal is against conviction, the Crown Court judge re-hears all the evidence that witnesses have already given in the lower court, but there is no jury. For all appeals the judge sits with two, three or four lay magistrates.

## County courts

Just as the magistrates' courts deal with the vast majority of criminal cases, those at the less serious end of the scale, county courts take on most of the smaller civil cases. In general, they deal with breach of contract or tort cases involving up to £5,000, which takes in the vast majority of civil actions. The courts deal mainly with claims for money – payment for goods sold, or fees for work done. They also hear repossession actions by building societies against mortgage defaulters (where the amount outstanding is not more than £30,000), disputes between landlord and tenant (mostly actions by landlords to get their property back), cases involving wills and estates up to £30,000 and winding up companies. Some courts also deal with bankruptcies.

Small claims, for under £500, are dealt with by a special procedure, designed to be quicker, cheaper and more informal than the normal (see Chapter I). County courts also have jurisdiction over most matrimonial matters. They can grant undefended divorces and make a range of orders relating to money, property and children; they have the power to order a violent husband or lover out of the home. There are county courts all over England and Wales, more than 270 altogether. The judges have the rank of circuit judge, the same level as those who sit in the Crown Court.

## The High Court

The High Court is a hotch-potch. It is a composite description embracing three separate kinds of court – called divisions – each with separate functions (though they occasionally overlap) and descended from an even greater confusion of ancient courts, going back to the twelfth century. The seventy-four High Court judges are distributed between the three divisions, which have their home in London's Royal Courts of Justice, an eccentric Victorian Gothic building on the Strand, with outposts in some twenty-five large provincial towns and cities.

The biggest of the divisions, with forty-six judges and the widest jurisdiction, is the Queen's Bench (King's Bench when the reigning monarch is male). Its most important function is as the main civil court for disputes involving more than £5,000. Claims for less than £5,000 may be started in the High Court, but if the amount eventually awarded is under £3,000, the judge will only award costs on the lower, county court, scale. A county court judge may transfer an action over a small amount of money to the High Court if it involves important issues of law or fact. In 1982, for example, Lord Bethell's action against the Belgian airline Sabena for over-charging him by £50 – part of his campaign to reduce European air fares – was transferred from Wandsworth county court to the High Court, at Sabena's request. Claims for money owing, and actions for damages arising from motor and factory accidents, are the High Court's main fodder. It also deals with suits for libel, which, though relatively few in number, frequently· get a lot of publicity because of the personalities involved. The division also includes a commercial court, which specialises in large commercial disputes, and an admiralty court for shipping cases.

The Divisional Court of the Queen's Bench Division (consisting of one, two or three judges depending on the type of case) provides one of the most important safeguards of a citizen's fundamental right to liberty in our society. The court can issue the famous and ancient writ of habeas corpus (literally, 'you have the body'), ordering the release of an individual who has been unlawfully detained, for instance by the police or by immigration authorities.

The Divisional Court's role as protector against abuse of power goes further. It is the main court of review for administrative decisions taken by bodies vested with some legal authority, such as government departments and local authorities. Challenges to such executive power are made under a procedure known as 'judicial review', which, following some well-publicized cases, has become an increasingly popular way of trying to contest controversial government and local council policies.

The court has shown that it is not frightened of finding ministerial decisions unlawful. It ruled, for instance, that the social services secretary, ·Norman Fowler, had no legal right to pass regulations withdrawing social security benefits from young people who stayed too long in lodgings. The transport secretary, Nicholas Ridley, is another who has had several Divisional Court rulings against his schemes. The judicial review procedure was also used by the Bar when they challenged the Lord Chancellor, Lord Hailsham's, decision over the level of criminal legal aid fees paid to barristers.

The court can also quash decisions of magistrates' courts where they exceed their powers or there are irregularities in the proceedings. It also takes appeals from lower courts, but only on issues raising points of law. The court does not hear witnesses or deal with cases which raise only factual points.

The Family Division is the next largest of the divisions of the High Court, with sixteen judges including its head, the President. The 'bleeding hearts' part of our judicial system, it deals with divorce; disputes between warring spouses involving children, property or money; adoption, wardship and other questions affecting children. Its judges belie the reputation of the judiciary for being behind the times, conservative and moralistic: they are often in the vanguard of progressive thinking on family matters.

The Chancery Division's twelve judges, plus its head, the Vice-Chancellor, deal with arid (to the outsider) but important areas of law such as tax, interpretation of wills, companies, settlements, trusts and various other issues affecting finance and property. It was the forerunner of the Chancery Division that fell victim to Charles Dickens' vitriolic pen in *Bleak House:*

> This is the Court of Chancery; which has its decaying houses and its blighted lands in every shire; which has its worn-out lunatic in every madhouse, and its dead in every churchyard; which has its ruined suitor, with his slipshod heels and threadbare dress, borrowing and begging through the round of every man's acquaintance; which gives to monied might the means abundantly of wearying out the right; which so exhausts finances, patience, courage, hope; so overthrows the brain and breaks the heart; that there is not an honourable man among its practitioners who would not give – who does not often give – the warning, 'Suffer any wrong that can be done you, rather than come here!'

Things have changed since, but the Chancery Division still retains a reputation for sluggish performance. In 1982, major reforms were introduced in an attempt to streamline its work.


## The Court of Appeal

The English legal system is in the fortunate, though perhaps unnecessary, position of having a two-tier system of appeals. The Court of Appeal is the main repository of dissatisfaction with the decisions of lower courts. Above it is the House of Lords.

In the Court of Appeal sit the judges who influence and form the law of England, perhaps even more than their superiors in the House of Lords. There are two divisions of the appeal court: the head of the Criminal Division is no less than the Lord Chief Justice, currently Lord Lane, the country's top judge. The Civil Division is led by the Master of the Rolls, now Sir John Donaldson. Until recently the office was held by Lord Denning, who retired at the age of eighty-three after twenty years in the job. It is yet another oddity of the system that these, the two most senior judges, do not sit in the most senior court, the House of Lords. The twenty-two Lords Justices of Appeal are at the centre of the law's development. When a written law is uncertain or leaves a gap, it has to be interpreted, and it is the three judges who sit on each appeal who set most of the precedents that have to be followed by the lower courts, and often make the newspaper headlines.

The Civil Division hears some 1,100 appeals a year, from the High Court as well as from county courts and a few more specialized courts. The Criminal Division, manned by High Court as well as appeal judges, deals with about 8,000 appeals, though most of them are against the sentence only. In contrast, the House of Lords in 1985 dealt with fewer than fifty appeals.

The Court of Appeal does not hear witnesses, other than in exceptional circumstances. The decisions are based on documents and transcripts, supplemented by the arguments of barristers, or sometimes of individuals who appear in person.

## The House of Lords

Even the name confuses. The House of Lords is, of course, Parliament's second chamber, made up of peers of the realm. But the term is also used as shorthand to describe those legal members of the House who hear appeals. Law lords, or, to give their formal title, Lords of Appeal in Ordinary, are eminent judges from English courts as well as Scottish. (The House of Lords is the final arbiter not only of all English law, but also of Scottish civil, though not criminal, law.) Constitutionally, the appeal is actually to the whole House of Lords and until the nineteenth century non-lawyer peers could and did sit, however much they lacked judicial ability. Only in 1876 was it formally provided that the job should be given over to experienced judges. But some remnants of the past remain. The law lords do not deliver judgments like all other judges, they make speeches. They do not come to a decision, they take a vote on a motion that the appeal be dismissed or allowed.

There are at any time between nine and eleven law lords, of whom two usually come from the Scottish judiciary; the Lord Chancellor and former Lord Chancellors are also entitled to sit. They sit in panels of five, in committee rooms in the Houses of Parliament at Westminster. The five elderly gentlemen wear ordinary dark suits and no wigs and they sit in a semi-circle behind a horseshoe table, not a raised dais or high platform. The discussion on fine points of law between the barristers and the law lords is carried out in low voices without histrionics.

There is no right to take an appeal to the House of Lords; permission to do so has to be given either by the Court of Appeal from whose decision the appeal is made, or by the House of Lords itself. In general, law lords will only hear cases involving points of law of public importance. They must have a significance going beyond the individuals involved in the case. Very rarely, the House of Lords can hear appeals directly from the High Court – 'leapfrogging' the Court of Appeal.

Why is the appeal to the House of Lords necessary? There is already a Court of Appeal manned by some of our best judges. Why another court? It seems an unnecessary luxury to have five appeal judges sitting in judgment on the decision of three scarcely (if at all) less able judges. And it can and does lead to absurd results. Where, for instance, the Court of Appeal has decided by three to nil in favour of one side and the House of Lords decides the other way by a margin of three to two, the judgment that becomes the law of the land has the support of only three out of eight of the best judges in the country. The costs of taking a case to one appeal, let alone to two, are prohibitive. There seems to be no logically convincing reason for retaining the double appeal option.

## Some other courts

The six mainstream courts described above do not by any means exhaust the list. A number of other, more specialized, courts have been set up to deal with particular areas of the law or perform special functions.

*The Judicial Committee of the Privy Council* is a relic of colonial times. In the days of the British Empire, the Privy Council sat at its centre, London, as the supreme court of appeal for all the colonies and dominions. Britain had provided those countries with a legal system, and it was natural that it should give them the opportunity to come before the most august judges of the motherland. As the Empire waned, so did the Privy Council's influence. Its jurisdiction is now confined to hearing appeals from the remaining colonies (with Hong Kong the most important), and from those former British territories which have chosen to retain it as their final appeal court. There is something strange about one sovereign country's giving the final right to rule on its laws to the judges of another, and many Commonwealth countries – Canada, India, Australia and most of the African states, for example – have found reference to the Privy Council to be incompatible with their independence. But some – among them Singapore, Malaysia, New Zealand, Jamaica and Trinidad – have chosen to retain it because they think it is no bad thing to have the chance of putting their difficult legal problems before judges who are still probably the most able in the world. The judges of the Privy Council are predominantly the same law lords that normally sit in the House of Lords, with the addition every now and again of eminent judges from Commonwealth countries.

*The Employment Appeal Tribunal* was set up following the great increase in recent years of disputes arising from employment, especially involving unfair dismissal or discrimination. The court hears appeals from industrial tribunals. Every case is heard by a High Court judge and two lay members chosen for their knowledge and experience of industrial relations: trade union officials, for instance, and representatives of employers' organizations.

*The Restrictive Practices Court,* which is of the level of the High Court, has various powers to stop or control restrictive or monopolistic practices in the supply of goods and services – for example, agreements between ostensibly competitive companies to charge a minimum price for their products, against the interests of the consumer.

*Coroners' Courts:* Coroners, who must be qualified lawyers or doctors, have a duty to hold public inquests into any violent, unnatural or suspicious death, or in the case of a person dying suddenly without any obvious cause, or in prison or in police custody. Coroners' inquests are not trials, but witnesses are called and there is often a jury who decide on the manner of death – suicide, unlawful killing, misadventure or accident – or (where they are not sure) return an open verdict.

## Tribunals

Outside the normal hierarchy of the courts flourishes a parallel structure of administrative and judicial bodies lumped together under the general description of tribunals. Some of them have been in existence for a century or more, but they have proliferated especially in the last thirty years, since the creation of the welfare state. The sixty or so tribunals cover a wide range of subjects, from tax to mental health, from forestry to patents. Some of the most important and widely used are the industrial tribunals, where workers can claim compensation for unfair dismissal; the supplementary benefit appeals tribunal; rent tribunals; and the immigration appeals tribunal.

The tribunals differ in their membership and rules of procedure, but they all conduct themselves according to the principles of justice used by the courts, especially in that the individuals appearing before them must have a chance to put their case. Unfortunately, legal aid is not available for hearings at most tribunals, which prevents many people from having legal representation and maximizing their chances of success.

## Two foreign courts

Two courts outside Britain's boundaries have recently come to play a big part in her affairs. The two deal with completely different issues, and belong to different regional institutions, but they are often confused in the public mind.

The European Court (more properly the Court of Justice of the European Communities) sits in Luxembourg. It is the court of the EEC, and therefore Britain, as a member, is under its jurisdiction on matters affecting the Community. Its decisions on the interpretation of Community law are the last word in that area of the law – superior even to the pronouncements of the House of Lords. Its rulings to date have mainly concerned issues important to the business world but it has also given decisions of great importance to individuals, such as its ruling that women had the right to go on working to the same retirement age as men.

The European Court of Human Rights sits in Strasbourg and operates under the umbrella of the Council of Europe, an organization with twenty-one member states. As its name suggests, the court deals with issues of human rights. It gives rulings on whether particular conduct by a government or one of its organs violates the European Convention on Human Rights, which Britain has signed. It has made a number of rulings against the British Government on the rights of mental patients, prisoners and immigrants; and on such diverse topics as the right not to be caned at school, and not to belong to a trade union. The court cannot be approached directly: all cases have to go first to the European Commission of Human Rights, and only a handful each year reach the court.

# CHAPTER III

# THE LAWYERS

To the rest of the world, the English legal profession is a very strange species indeed. Most countries manage to do with one kind of lawyer. We, and a few other places which historically came under our influence, have two. Barristers and solicitors are usually thought of – and speak of themselves – as the two branches of a single legal profession. On closer examination, they really function as two separate professions, with different traditions, training and rules of conduct, and administered by separate governing bodies, but with a common body of knowledge, the law, and a common arena of operation, the courts.

Why two kinds of lawyer? As with so many of the legal profession's odd quirks, the reason for the division is historical, but it now suits both branches of the profession to maintain it, as proof against encroachment on each other's work.

The forerunners of today's barristers and solicitors were a mixed bunch, with varying titles and functions over the centuries. As long ago as the thirteenth century there were lawyers whose job was to plead in the King's courts on behalf of litigants, and court officials who acted as 'attorneys', providing general help to people involved in court proceedings, including appearing in court. Pleaders (barristers and serjeants) and attorneys both pleaded in court and both received clients direct. After lawyers organized themselves into the Inns of Court in the mid-fourteenth century, there was a gradual separation of functions. Eventually attorneys were excluded from the Inns, and the higher courts came to be reserved for barristers and serjeants. In the meantime, other types of lawyers had appeared on the scene. Solicitors were concerned with property work and the chancery courts. Cases in chancery could drag on for generations, and the only way of moving matters forward was to employ someone to 'solicit' or cajole the court into getting on with things. Yet another legal functionary, the proctor, operated in the ecclesiastical and admiralty courts.

At first the solicitor was considered inferior to the attorney, but gradually their relative status was reversed, as solicitors' responsibility for land dealings made them the trusted advisers of the powerful land-owning class. In 1875 the functions of solicitors, proctors and attorneys were merged, and the single title of solicitor was adopted. Serjeants were abolished too, leaving only barristers to represent that branch of the profession.

## BARRISTERS

The Bar is the most traditional of professions. What other profession requires its practitioners to spend much of their working lives kitted out in period costume? In London, barristers still occupy the same offices (called 'chambers') in the Inns of Court – Gray's Inn, Lincoln's Inn, the Inner Temple and the Middle Temple – which have housed them since the fourteenth century, even though the lack of space prevents able youngsters from entering the profession and forces senior practitioners to work two or three to a room. No one can qualify as a barrister without eating the required number of dinners in his Inn, a tradition dating from Elizabethan times, before the introduction of formal legal education, when the theory was that the embryo lawyer would imbibe his elders' experience along with the equally well-aged claret.

Solicitors, accountants, surveyors and other lesser mortals may sue clients who are recalcitrant in paying their fees. Not so the barrister. Historically, the barrister worked not for a fee, but for an 'honorarium'. Hence the pocket flap which still survives at the back of the barrister's gown, into which at one time the satisfied client would slip a token of his gratitude, without ever having to raise the sordid subject of money in conversation.

Practice at the Bar is governed by an assortment of such customs, conventions and rules of etiquette of varying degrees of antiquity. Take the two main distinctions between barristers and solicitors: the rule that a barrister's clients can only come to him via a solicitor, and the restriction which allows only barristers to argue cases before the higher courts. Contrary to popular belief, the first of these dictats is a relatively recent development, only enshrined in a rule in the late nineteenth century. Until then, barristers could be consulted by clients directly, though by the beginning of the nineteenth century it had become the custom to approach a barrister only through a solicitor.

The second rule – that only barristers can appear before the Crown Court, High Court, and appeal courts – evolved from an old common law rule that the courts can decide for themselves who may appear before them, and by convention the higher courts reserved the right for barristers. Even now, in a few Crown Courts in areas where there is no local Bar, solicitors have equal 'rights of audience' (the right to conduct cases before the court) with barristers. Bodmin Crown Court in Cornwall is one such anomaly.

The Bar is regulated by a strict code of conduct. One of the most important principles is known as the 'cab-rank rule'. This is meant to ensure that everyone who needs a lawyer – even the most unpopular IRA terrorist or child molester – should have someone to champion his cause. Broadly, it says that a barrister must take any case he is offered, as long as it is within his usual sphere of practice, he is not otherwise engaged, and a proper fee is tendered.

Who are the barristers, and what distinguishes them from solicitors? Barristers are largely drawn from the middle and upper-middle classes. One quarter of the Bar students replying to a 1976 survey had family connections with the law. Solicitors' backgrounds are also largely middle-class, but there is a wider spread of social class origin among solicitors, who outnumber the 5,300 practising barristers in England and Wales by nine to one. Though many solicitors, particularly in the large London firms, share the Bar's mainly public school/Oxbridge background, the Bar still considers itself an intellectual and social élite.

Officially, though, it no longer describes itself as the 'senior' branch of the profession: in 1973 the Chairman of the Bar and the President of The Law Society (the solicitors' professional body) issued a joint statement announcing that the two branches were of equal status if of differing functions. But status is not so easily conferred, and although solicitors undergo the same sort of education (the solicitors' professional examination is reckoned to be the more rigorous of the two, and the period of practical training a year longer), and enjoy similar levels of financial reward, historical vestiges of the barrister's superiority still remain. The solicitor who wants a barrister's advice must always go to the barrister – only exceptionally will a barrister set foot in a solicitor's office. High court judgeships, the plums at the top of the professional tree, are reserved for barristers. Apart from cases of 'special difficulty', barristers do not negotiate their fees directly with solicitors. Fees are discussed with the barrister's clerk, and all correspondence is addressed to the barrister through his clerk.

In recent years the acute shortage of openings at the Bar and the uncertain level of earnings in the first few years have frightened many high-quality graduates who might otherwise have gone to the Bar into opting for the greater security of the solicitors' branch. Recent research has shown fewer Oxbridge first class law graduates becoming barristers and more becoming solicitors. While in the early 1950s 38 per cent went to the Bar and only 14 per cent became solicitors, 45 per cent of 1977 graduates went into practice as solicitors, and only 28 per cent as barristers.

To qualify as a barrister – to be 'called to the bar' – now normally needs at least a second class degree, though not necessarily in law. The would-be barrister joins one of the Inns of Court, and has to dine there three times in each quarterly 'dining term' for two years, although it is often possible to compress the twenty-four dinners into one year.

The crucial year is the one in which he takes the Bar examinations and goes through a vocational training course at the Inns of Court School of Law. During their vocational year aspiring barristers participate in mock trials and advocacy exercises conducted by experienced barristers. The training is run on modern lines, contrary to the old-fashioned image the profession presents. Television and audio-visual aids play an essential part. Nothing so draws attention to the young student's inadequacies as seeing himself mumbling and bumbling on a large television screen in the company of his fellow students and a critical senior barrister. The vocational course includes lectures and seminars dealing with the more practical aspects of his work rather than the law itself.

Passing the Bar exams and being called to the Bar are just the beginning. A barrister who wants to practise at the Bar must do twelve months 'pupillage' in chambers, sitting in on conferences with his 'pupil master' (a more senior barrister), following him around to court, looking up points of law, doing some paperwork, and generally learning the tricks of the trade. Pupillages are unpaid, but during the second six months the young barrister may take on work of his own – if he is lucky enough to get any. Pupillage is not accepted by everyone as the best means of introducing a new barrister into the profession. It is a somewhat hit-and-miss method. But some objections are on different grounds. Lord Gifford QC, a barrister on the radical wing of the profession, believes that pupillage is in practice only open to those who can afford not to earn any money for a year or so:

> So you have an enormous bias towards those who have private means . This is bad for the students and the pupils, but it's bad for the public interest as well, because the people who become barristers in the first place, twenty years later become QCs and judges, and have an enormous effect upon our public life. And therefore the public should be demanding that they are chosen in the beginning on some kind of rational basis, which they're not.

A second criticism is that pupillage is insecure, because there is no guarantee that the pupil will be able to stay in the same chambers after his year is over. The barrister can only practise if he is offered a 'seat' or 'tenancy' in a set of chambers. In recent years, the number of candidates has outstripped the vacancies available by more than two to one. A young barrister may be allowed to 'squat' in chambers at the end of his pupillage, doing any work which comes his way, and hoping for the chance of a tenancy. Eventually, many are forced to abandon the Bar, taking jobs in business, the civil service or outside the law, or switching over to the solicitors' branch.

It is certainly true that in the past getting a pupillage or a seat in chambers was a question of who you knew rather than what you knew – connections rather than merit. Young barristers argue that this is still the case, but the Bar claims that in recent years it has done everything it can – through scholarships, loans, competitive interviews – to ensure that getting on to the first rung depends on ability, not contacts. An increasing number of chambers now provide bursaries for pupils. Lord Gifford doesn't think this goes nearly far enough. In his chambers, they advertise widely for pupils, pay them a living wage, and guarantee that they can join the chambers when the year of pupillage ends. But this is very much the exception.

Even the fortunate few who secure tenancies can by no means look forward to an assured future. Every barrister is a self-employed, independent operator. Unlike the newly-qualified solicitor, who is paid a salary and given work by the partners in his firm, the fledgling barrister is expected to attract his own work and earn his own fees. In practice, he will rely heavily on the clerk to the chambers to suggest his name to solicitors ringing up to ask for someone appropriate to handle simple county court and magistrates' court work, and to persuade solicitors to substitute him when their first choice turns out to be otherwise engaged. Distinguished judges are fond of recalling how they were on the verge of leaving the Bar in desperation when the brief (the document by which solicitors hire barristers) came in that changed their luck. The coming of legal aid, however, has relegated the briefless barrister to the ranks of fiction, and public funds now provide a cushion against penury in the first few years.

## Women

The proportion of women at the Bar is about 13 per cent, but growing every year. Women account for nearly 40 per cent of the students at the Inns of Court School of Law. Women barristers seem to find pupillages just as readily as their male counterparts, but tenancies are harder to come by. Some clerks and heads of chambers are believed to operate a quota system: they claim that solicitors don't like briefing women barristers, or that women will let the chambers down by going off to start families. Few sets of chambers have more than two women, and many still have none. Female barristers find themselves channelled into divorce and crime, the least intellectually challenging areas of work, and they tend to earn less than their male colleagues.

## The specialist advocate?

A medical analogy is often used to explain the difference between barristers and solicitors, with the barrister as the consultant and the solicitor the general practitioner. In fact, the analogy is no more than a half-truth. Barristers work mostly either in 'common law' (generalist), Chancery or specialist chambers. Barristers with a common law practice (which includes most of the 1,500 barristers outside London) do a mixture of work: crime, contract, personal injuries, landlord and tenant, divorce. There are specializations within those ranges – chambers that do only crime, or divorce or libel. Chancery barristers deal with areas such as trusts, wills and probate, land, bankruptcy, company law and tax. There are also specialist chambers for libel, planning, tax, local government, shipping, employment, patents, and commercial law. Looking at the Bar as a whole, only a small proportion of barristers could be said to specialize in a particular field to the extent that they do little else.

The Bar describes itself as a cadre of specialist advocates. But, unlike the medical specialists' claim to expertise, the Bar's is not based on a rigorous programme of extra study and training. There is much more training in advocacy than there used to be but, even so, the newly-called barrister has far less claim to the title of specialist advocate than the experienced solicitor who has appeared hundreds of times before the magistrates' and county courts. The barrister's claim to be a specialist in High Court, Crown Court and appeal court advocacy rests on his monopoly of advocacy in those courts. Solicitors actually do more advocacy than barristers, though only in the lower courts, where both have the right to appear. For every person represented in court by a barrister, nine are represented by solicitors.

## The brief

Since no one can retain a barrister's services except through a solicitor, a barrister relies for his work on what solicitors send him. Solicitors tend to have their favourite sets of chambers for particular types of work. When a case finally comes to court, only a barrister can represent the client in the higher courts. In the county court or magistrates' court, a solicitor has the choice of acting as advocate himself or instructing a barrister. Practical considerations will decide which he chooses. If he has a string of clients appearing before the local magistrates on the same day, it might be more economical to represent them all himself. On the other hand, if a case involves an appearance before a distant county court, it might be cheaper to send along a young barrister, who will do it for a flat fee, almost certainly less than a solicitor would have to charge for his own time. In most cases, the barrister's rules of etiquette prevent him from appearing in court alone without the attendance of a member of the solicitor's staff, though this rule has been modified for simple cases in magistrates' courts. Further relaxation of the rule is under discussion.

The means of communication between solicitor and barrister is the brief, the document which tells the barrister what the solicitor wants him to do, and gives him all the information he needs to do the job. The barrister may be briefed to appear in court, or to give an opinion on a tricky point of law, or to draft pleadings (documents used in civil cases) or to advise on whether to accept an offer of settlement.

The brief to appear for the defence in a criminal trial is also the cause of one of the main criticisms about the system, the late return of briefs. Barristers operate by a cab-rank rule. Like taxi-drivers they can't pick and choose their clients, nor even which side they are on. But because one trial will end earlier than expected and another will go on much longer, a clerk will often double-book a barrister, rather as travel agencies or airlines overbook, to make sure that he isn't left with an empty, and hence unpaid-for, day. The briefs that the barristers can't handle then have to be returned to be reallocated, usually to another member of the chambers who happens to be free – sometimes to someone more junior. Perhaps as many as one-third of briefs are returned in this way, and sometimes the return is made very late – the evening before the trial. All this may seem sensible and efficient from the Bar's point of view, but it can be a disaster for the client. He has been told by his solicitor that a particular barrister is appearing on his behalf, and comes to court to find another. Often he believes – sometimes justifiably – that the new counsel foisted on him is inferior, and doesn't properly know the case. It leads to bitterness and loss of confidence in the system of justice. Richard Du Cann QC, a former chairman of the Bar:

> It's a matter of bitter regret to the Bar that they cannot, because of the way the system operates, meet all the demands which are put upon them. I'm afraid it's inevitable where you get the system organized on the basis that the court will fix the date of the trial of a case according to the convenience of the calendar of the court, instead of the convenience of the client and the convenience of the advocate who is involved.

The difficulty is caused by the system of listing cases for trial. To make maximum use of court time, the listing officials have to show great flexibility in juggling cases around. This means that a barrister often gets only a day or two's notice of the day of the trial, and he may be involved in another case.

The relationship between solicitor and barrister largely excludes the individual client. He cannot see or contact the barrister directly, only through his solicitor. Occasionally there is a meeting – a conference – between the client, his solicitor and his barrister, but only if the case is complicated or the barrister feels the brief is inadequate. Most defendants in criminal cases do not meet their barristers until the day of the trial. Research shows that 96 per cent of those pleading guilty and 79 per cent of those pleading not guilty only meet their barristers on the morning of the trial. Richard Du Cann QC answers:

> If the preliminary work has been done by the solicitor, as it needs to be, with care and with thoroughness, there is a very high proportion of cases where it isn't necessary for a meeting to take place. The need for the barrister to master the facts is in many cases independent from meeting the client.

That may be so, but it is often not appreciated by the client, and Richard Du Cann is conscious that clients are increasingly going to want to have meetings with the lawyer entrusted with arguing their case in court.

## Earnings

A barrister's earnings will increase as he gains experience and takes on more weighty work, though how much he earns will depend on his own ability, how hard he is willing to work, and the area of law he practices in. Barristers are divided into two tiers: QCs (Queen's Counsel) and juniors. All barristers who are not QCs are called juniors, regardless of their age or seniority. The successful junior, after around fifteen to twenty years' practice, may apply to become a QC or 'take silk' (so called because the QC wears a silk gown). Forty-eight new silks were appointed in 1986, around one-fifth of those who applied. Some are turned down several times before they make it, others never succeed and eventually stop applying. The process of selection is carried out by the Lord Chancellor and his permanent secretary in consultation with the most senior judges, leading barristers, and the law officers. It operates in much the same way as the method of choosing High Court judges (see Chapter IV).

QCs are the top 10 per cent of the profession – there are fewer than 600 of them – and they form the pool from which most High Court judges are drawn. Taking silk brings increased status, higher fees, and the chance to get rid of a heavy load of paperwork. A QC appearing in court will almost always have a junior helping him.

Until 1977, the Bar's rules of conduct prevented a QC from working without a junior. Although the rule has been dropped, following a Monopolies Commission finding that it was against the public interest, most QCs still claim that they need a junior's assistance. So not only will the client have to pay the higher fees due to a QC, he will have to pay for two barristers instead of one. The risk in taking silk is that not enough clients will want to pay so much more, and a previously flourishing career may stagnate. But the few fashionable silks in heavy demand can earn considerably more than £100,000 a year. A handful are reputed to gross over half a million pounds.

In 1982, the Top Salaries Review Body published the results of a survey of earnings of both QCs and juniors in the age bracket where they might expect to be appointed judges. Among QCs, the top half of earners doing chancery work (which includes trusts, wills, and land law) averaged £67,000. The top 50 per cent of common law silks practising in London earned between £43,000 and £61,000, and London specialist silks between £60,000 and £87,000.

At the other end, the Bar complains, barristers doing publicly funded criminal work are poorly paid, and the Bar recently took the unprecedented step of taking the Lord Chancellor to court over his decision to limit legal aid fee rises to 5 per cent. The court was sympathetic to the barristers' plight, and the case was settled after the Lord Chancellor promised proper negotiations with the Bar on legal aid fees. A 1985 survey showed median earnings after expenses of only £8,620 in 1983/4 for a London criminal barrister of 10 to 15 years' experience. A mixture of civil and criminal work produced a median income of £15,700 in London, and a middle-earning provincial barrister called between 10 and 15 years netted £19,270 before tax.

## Organization

Unlike solicitors, barristers are not allowed to practise in partnership or share fees. Each barrister remains an independent contractor of his own services. But for convenience – and because of tradition – they cluster together in sets of chambers containing an average of about fifteen members.

In London, chambers are concentrated in the four Inns of Court: Lincoln's Inn, Gray's Inn, Inner Temple and Middle Temple. The chambers belong to the Inns and are rented to the sets of barristers at below market rent. Each set has its head, usually a senior QC, and is administered by a clerk. The members contribute, often in proportion to their earnings, to running expenses, rent, heat and light, typists' salaries and clerks' fees. Barristers' overheads generally work out at around one-third of their gross fees (compared with the solicitors' two-thirds).

No one knows exactly when the four Inns of Court were

established, but they were already a going concern in the fourteenth century. Originally medieval guilds of lawyers, they appear to have served as residential clubs for lawyers and places where students came to learn the law. Stepping from the bustle of Fleet Street into the courtyards and lawns of the Temple is like taking a trip backwards in time. Though some of the buildings are post-war, rebuilt following bomb damage, the new blends inconspicuously with the old, leaving an impression of a beautiful but cloistered and anachronistic world. Lord Gifford, whose chambers are an exception, located not in the Inns but in an ordinary office building in Covent Garden, finds the atmosphere of the Inns attractive but 'very corrupting':

> Barristers who operate from London spend their whole working life either in that little precinct, that little enclave of the Inns of Court, or they go into courts which themselves are very artificial theatres, cut off from the real world. And when you think that a number of the people we're talking about have spent their early life anyway in some way set apart – they may have been to public schools or they may have been to an old university – it enhances this feeling that we are something special, something above the rest, some special breed of being.

Every student has to join an Inn, and he remains a member of that Inn throughout his life at the Bar and on the bench, if he becomes a judge. Members lunch and dine in their Inns and use their libraries. It is the Benchers (governing members) of the Inns who call a student to the Bar.

Barristers practising outside London are much less cloistered. They tend to be grouped together in smaller chambers, in run of the mill office buildings near the court, not set apart from the rest in their own little world.

The Bar Council is the barristers' elected representative body. It sets the standards and ethics of professional conduct, and represents generally the interests of its members – the nearest equivalent of a trade union for barristers. The Senate of the Inns of Court and the Bar is the profession's overall governing and policy-making body. At the time of writing a change to a single governing body seemed likely.

## Complaints against barristers

Far fewer complaints are made against barristers than against solicitors, reflecting the fact that the great bulk of legal work is handled by solicitors. Most complaints about barristers relate to their conduct of cases in court. Complaints are investigated by a committee of the Bar Council, with a lay member present. If a complaint is upheld, the committee may admonish the barrister or report him to his Inn. If the charge is a serious one, proceedings can be brought before the Disciplinary Tribunal of the Senate, which can impose a range of penalties culminating in ordering the barrister to be disbarred. The Bar Council and the Disciplinary Tribunal deal with complaints of incompetence as well as misconduct. They cannot order compensation to be paid to the client, but the Disciplinary Tribunal can order the barrister to repay (or forgo) his fees if he has acted improperly in a case.

Like solicitors, barristers can be sued for negligence in out-of-court work, but neither a solicitor nor a barrister can be sued over his performance as an advocate in court.

## Barristers' clerks

The senior barristers' clerk is a powerful figure, 'a complicated cross between a theatrical agent, a business manager, an accountant, and a trainer', in the words of Sir Robert Megarry, the head of the Chancery Division. The clerk negotiates the barrister's fees and to a large extent can make or break the career of the young barrister by diverting work to him or away from him. In many chambers the clerk will have a say in whether or not a new member is taken on. The Senate, the Bar's governing body, said in its evidence to the Royal Commission on Legal Services:

> There are still a few members of the Bar who would not take a day off without their clerk's approval (which might well not be granted), whose efforts to get him to collect their fees are ineffective and who can almost be regarded more as their clerk's man than their own.

Yet the clerk has no legal qualifications, and in most cases will have begun straight from school as a junior clerk, carrying books and running errands, gradually working his way up to a position of power and influence – and a level of earnings – out of all proportion to his academic attainments. Most clerks are paid on a commission basis, a percentage of the gross fees of the barristers they serve. The percentage varies between 5 and 10 per cent, with the clerks earning the higher percentage usually contributing a proportion of chambers' expenses out of their earnings. Criminal barristers surveyed in 1985 paid clerks' fees averaging about 7.5 per cent of their gross fees.

The incentive to exact as high a fee as possible for the barristers' services is obvious. One striking fact emerging from the report of the Royal Commission on Legal Services was that senior clerks often earn more than most of the barristers they work for. Clerks earning £30,000 a year or more are quite usual. In 1979, the average London set of chambers had 15 members, and some sets have as many as 30. A clerk on a straight 10 per cent commission in a set of 15 members would earn one and half times the average earnings of the barristers in his chambers.

Few sets of chambers have managed to put their clerks on a salary (only 8 per cent of clerks surveyed for the Royal Commission were on salary). The chambers headed by Sir Michael Havers QC, the Attorney-General, sacked their clerk in 1977 when he refused to agree to a reduction from 10 per cent (which left him £29,500 after paying the junior clerks' salaries) to 8 per cent. His claim of unfair dismissal failed. The Royal Commission recommended that the percentage basis of payment should be dropped, and all barristers' clerks paid a salary.

# SOLICITORS

It is a common fallacy that barristers spend all their time arguing in court while solicitors stay in their offices doing paperwork. Although perhaps as many as one in four of the 46,000 or so practising solicitors rarely ventures inside a courtroom, others spend half or more of their working week in court. Conversely, some barristers spend the bulk of their time on paperwork.

## What they do

As a high street practitioner, and first port of call for anyone with a legal problem, the average solicitor deals with a greater variety of work than the average barrister. Even when a barrister is involved in a case, most of the legal work is done by the solicitor. In a civil case, which may or may not go to court – such as a claim for damages for injuries in an accident – the solicitor does most of the preparatory work and conducts the negotiations which may lead to a settlement out of court. The barrister is called in by the solicitor to draft the court paperwork, to advise (particularly on whether or not an offer of settlement should be accepted), and to appear in court if the case gets that far.

Most criminal cases are handled from start to finish by solicitors in the magistrates' court, though some solicitors, particularly in London, make it a practice to instruct a junior barrister for the court hearing. More serious crimes are tried in the Crown Court, where the solicitor has only a limited right to appear. But even these cases start in the magistrates' court, from which the accused is committed for trial to the higher court. Committal proceedings in the magistrates' court, and any other applications there (for example, for bail) may be dealt with by either a barrister or a solicitor. The courts, though, are just the tip of the legal iceberg. Much legal work never, or rarely, involves the courts. Solicitors divide their work into 'contentious work' and 'non-contentious work'. Anything which involves court proceedings is contentious; examples include crime, divorce, and civil litigation (such as claims for damages in accident cases). Everything else is non-contentious.

Until recently, the less profitable contentious work was heavily subsidized by non-contentious, particularly conveyancing, which traditionally provided 50 per cent of the average firm's income. But moves in Parliament to smash the solicitor's monopoly on conveyancing work and open it up to non-lawyers – culminating in legislation allowing the licensing of conveyancers without legal qualifications – have resulted in fierce competition in the conveyancing market and brought fees down sharply. Solicitors have cut their margins to compete not only with the unqualified conveyancers, who as a result have not made great inroads into the solicitors' traditional preserve, but more particularly with each other. The Law Society's 1985 survey on the structure and finances of the legal profession found that the average firm now derives only about 30 per cent of its income from the conveyancing of houses and flats, as opposed to over 50 per cent in earlier surveys. One typical country solicitor practising in Sussex reports that his average conveyancing bill in early 1986 was only two-thirds as much as his average bill for the same period two years previously, despite the rise in house prices over that period. Solicitors complain that the low levels of payment for legal aid work have squeezed their profit margins in this traditionally low-profit field even further. Particularly badly off, according to the Law Society survey, are firms which rely heavily on criminal legal aid fees. For example, sole practitioners in the survey who drew over 30 per cent of their income from criminal legal aid averaged only £9,400 a year net profit as against £20,500 for those who took on no such work.

Most firms act as general practitioners or family solicitors, dealing with the complete range of their clients' legal problems, but calling in specialist advice when necessary. Within a three partner firm, the partners will specialize to some extent. A possible division of labour would have one partner doing conveyancing and probate, another conveyancing and work for business, and a third partner handling all the criminal work, civil litigation, and divorce.

## Structure and earnings

Solicitors practise on their own or in partnership, though for the first few years of his working life a solicitor usually works as a salaried or 'assistant' solicitor. The Law Society's rules prohibit a solicitor from setting up on his own for three years after admission. Solicitors are not allowed to incorporate themselves as limited companies, and each partner is fully liable for the debts or negligent acts of the other partners.

Partnerships range in size from two to seventy-plus, but 80 per cent of firms have four or fewer partners and one in three of the 7,500 firms in England and Wales is a one-man operation. The average firm in the Law Society's 1985 remuneration survey had three partners. A partner whose share of profits was right in the middle of the range for two-to-four partner firms would have earned £17,900. The middle of the sole practitioners' range was £20,400.

At the other extreme are a number of City of London firms with thirty or more partners and up to three times as many assistant solicitors. A half-dozen or so have over sixty partners. These firms serve the legal needs of big business: the conveyancing of office blocks, large scale town and country planning, business disputes involving large sums of money, company flotations and takeovers, tax, Eurobanking, and so on. Each partner and assistant solicitor is highly specialized. In the Law Society's survey, the median earnings for partners in central London firms with fifteen or more was £81,300 – four times the median for other firms. The top 10 per cent of partners in the big central London firms were pulling in more than £170,000 a year. A highly experienced assistant solicitor can earn £25,000 or more. The big provincial cities all have firms which do similar work, although on a smaller scale, and partners' earnings are lower – £38,500 average for firms with fifteen plus partners. In most of the larger towns, the one or two biggest firms will handle most of the legal work for local businesses. Businesses generate a lot of work for solicitors: setting up new companies, drafting contracts, acquiring new premises, dealing with employees – all have legal implications. London also has a number of medium-sized (ten to twenty partners) specialist firms (practising in such fields as insurance, shipping, libel and copyright, and trade union work) and similar-sized old established, upper-crust family firms. The work of solicitors, especially in the City, brings in around £80 million a year in foreign earnings through advising international clients.

The typical solicitor is likely to be under forty (the profession is bottom-heavy), white, male, and the product of a middle-class home. The usual route into the profession is through a law degree. Although a degree of any sort is not compulsory, about 98 per cent of entrants are graduates, not all in law. For the law graduate there is a further one year's practical course and examination. The non-law graduate needs an extra year on top of that.

Post-university training, once largely a cramming exercise conducted on rote-learning lines, has recently been overhauled. Trainees no longer arrive to serve their apprenticeships in solicitors' offices never having seen a legal document of any description. Now, during their course for the final exam, they taste the paperwork –

witness statements, partnership deeds, leases, writs and so on – which will be the meat and drink of their working lives.

The aspiring solicitor serves for at least two years as an articled clerk in a solicitor's office, during which he earns a small salary. During this time, he progresses from carrying out simple research, one-off drafting tasks, and 'supporting counsel' (sitting behind a barrister in court) to seeing his own cases through from start to finish. Most newly qualified solicitors find jobs, often with the firm in which they served articles.

Once the assistant solicitor has proved himself, he can hope to be offered a partnership. This means that he will get a share of the firm's profits instead of a salary. The median salary for assistant solicitors in April 1985 was £9,600, according to the Law Society's remuneration survey. Those working in firms of 15 or more partners did better, with a median of £13,000. The length of time it takes to become a partner will depend on luck, ability and the part of the country in which a solicitor practises. Outside London he should make it within five years: in some areas much sooner. In the big London firms, thirty-five is reckoned to be the make or break age for a partnership. Those who fail to make the grade generally move to a smaller firm with better partnership prospects, or reconcile themselves to remaining as assistant solicitors, consoled by their relatively high salaries and challenging work.

All the partners in the typical firm are male. Women make up only 17 per cent of the practising profession, though the picture is changing rapidly. One in three solicitors under 35 is a woman, and 40 per cent of solicitors admitted in 1985 were female. In the past, women have experienced difficulties in obtaining partnerships ('they'll just go off and have babies'), but this too is changing, and most of the large London firms now have at least one woman partner.

Once established in practice, the typical solicitor is likely to be overworked. A study of West Midlands solicitors by sociologist David Podmore (*Solicitors and the Wider Community,* Heinemann, 1980) found that one-quarter of the sample took work home three, four or more times a week. About the average solicitor's working day, Podmore comments: 'Typically, he operates under some pressure and deals with many different problems each working day. Few of the 103 inteviews with solicitors in private practice that were carried out in this research were not interrupted by urgent telephone calls.'

In recent years, solicitors have felt the pinch as competition has cut profits from conveyancing and rates of pay for legal aid work have failed to keep paced with rising office overheads, which eat up around two-thirds of fees earned. Solicitors do less well financially than do barristers, doctors, accountants and bank managers, according to the Law Society's 1985 survey.

Outside private practice, the Law Society estimates that

somewhere in the region of 6,000 men and women are employed as solicitors in commerce and industry, and in central and local government. Building societies, finance houses, insurance companies, property companies and large companies of all sorts increasingly employ in-house lawyers in the American mould, to advise the company on the legality of its proposed activities, do its conveyancing and litigation, act as company secretaries, and brief lawyers in private practice where necessary. Solicitors in local government provide a similar sort of service to the elected council. The chief executive of a local authority is often a solicitor, and company lawyers often move into management. Solicitors in industry do better financially than those in private practice, taking into account pensions and other perks which the solicitor in private practice has to provide out of his earnings.

## Legal executives

Legal executives are the non-commissioned officers of the solicitors' branch. The successors to the nineteenth-century managing clerks, they handle the more routine legal work, particularly conveyancing, divorce, probate and litigation. They see clients and carry cases through from start to finish under the nominal supervision of partners. The Royal Commission on Legal Services noted that 30 per cent of conveyancing work was done by legal executives and articled clerks.

Most firms have at least one legal executive. The Institute of Legal Executives guesses that as many as 20,000 legal executives work in solicitors' offices, some qualified by the Institute's exams, others only by experience. But with the influx of new solicitors the trend is for more of the routine work to be taken over by assistant solicitors.

## Organization

The Law Society is the solicitors' professional association, which seeks to advance the interests of the profession. Membership is voluntary; some 80 per cent of practising solicitors are members. But the Society has much wider functions, and controls the education of solicitors, their admission to the profession, and their right to practise. To obtain the annual practising certificate – the licence to practise issued by the Law Society – a solicitor must be insured under the Society's compulsory professional negligence scheme and file an annual accountant's report.

## Complaints against solicitors

The Law Society sets its own rules of conduct, including strict rules about the handling of clients' money, and administers penalties for lapses. As part of its disciplinary function, the Society deals with complaints from the public about solicitors. Examples of the sort of behaviour the Law Society will look at are: delay; persistent failure to answer letters; acting for two clients with conflicting interests; dishonesty; misleading the court; taking unfair advantage of a client (for instance, persuading a suggestible elderly lady to leave the solicitor something in her will).

If the complaint is found to be justified, the Society can reprimand the solicitor, or decide that he can only practise subject to certain conditions – for example, only with a partner. For serious offences, such as misusing clients' money, proceedings may be brought before the independent Solicitors' Disciplinary Tribunal, which can impose more severe punishments, including striking off the roll of solicitors. The client, however, gets no compensation unless he loses money through a solicitor's (or his employee's) dishonesty, in which case the Law Society's compensation fund will make good the loss.

What the Royal Commission on Legal Services described as 'a general feeling of unease about the Law Society's handling of complaints, a feeling that "lawyers look after their own"' led the Society to decide, in 1986, to split off the investigation of complaints by setting up a Solicitors' Complaints Bureau. The Bureau, which the Society hopes will be operational in 1987, will be part of the Law Society but will be housed in a separate building. Complaints will be investigated initially by an Investigation Committee, chaired by a non-solicitor and with a majority of lay members, and will be referred for action to the Adjudication Committee, which will have a majority of solicitor members. In serious cases, proceedings will still be brought before the Solicitors' Disciplinary Tribunal.

Traditionally, the Law Society has always refused to take on complaints about a solicitor's incompetence or negligence unless the behaviour also amounted to professional misconduct. However, from 1987, under powers given it by the Administration of Justice Act, the Society will look at complaints of shoddy work and will be able to order a solicitor who does a bad job to hand back his fees or to rectify his mistakes. Negligence, the Society has always maintained, is a matter for the courts; it has no machinery for testing the evidence and no power to make a solicitor pay compensation. If a complaint seems to be alleging negligence, the client will be advised to take advice from an independent solicitor. However, in response to complaints that dissatisfied clients have had difficulty in finding a solicitor willing to sue another solicitor, the Society has set up a negligence panel of experienced solicitors who will give a free initial interview, and advise on the strength of the case. If it is worth pursuing, the solicitor will take it on himself or refer it to a colleague. Legal aid is available for anyone who qualifies financially. All solicitors are insured against negligence claims, and well over 90 per cent are settled out of court.

In 1986, the Chartered Institute of Arbitrators set up, at the Law Society's request, an arbitration scheme designed to be used as an alternative to court proceedings for smaller negligence claims.

## WHY A DIVIDED PROFESSION?

What is the justification for having the legal profession divided into two branches, with solicitors and barristers prepared for their professional examinations in different institutions, trained and apprenticed separately, organized professionally in their distinctive ways and responsible to different bodies, each with its own customs and code of behaviour? Most other countries in the world, after all, manage perfectly well with only one kind of lawyer. Why do we need two? More importantly, does such a two-tier structure serve the interests of justice, and the interests of those members of the public who find themselves involved in the legal system?

The theoretical justification for a two-tier profession is that one branch provides a service that is different from, or better than, anything offered by the other. The claim made for the Bar, as we have said, is that it is the specialist branch – its members are specialists in advocacy, or in a particular area of the law. They make their expert services available to solicitors, who lack the necessary ability or expertise. That is the theory. How far does it accord with the reality?

The answer is mixed. There are barristers who, through cumulative day-to-day experience in the courts, become experts at trial advocacy. But they don't start off that way. Young barristers now get some training in advocacy, though not nearly enough to describe them as specialists in it. Some never become very good at it. By contrast, there are many solicitors who spend most of their time in advocacy in the lower courts and become thoroughly skilled. To suggest that barristers are, and solicitors are not, specialists in advocacy is therefore misleading. Equally, while many barristers do acquire, over the years, an expert knowledge of a particular area of the law, many solicitors can claim similar experience and expertise.

Another of the justifications for the present structure is that it provides a pool of specialists to which any solicitor, however small his firm or lowly his clientele, can go for expert advice or advocacy in court. It means, in theory, that every client has at his command the best legal brains and skills in the land. In practice, the choice is far more limited, and the degree of specialization is not always high, but the general principle is valid.

### Disadvantages

Critics of the system say that the division in the legal profession, and especially the rule restricting rights of audience in the higher courts to barristers, necessarily means duplication of effort, which in turn results in duplication of costs and therefore higher fees, and often leads to delay and inefficiency. As Michael Zander, Professor of Law at the London School of Economics and one of the leading advocates for change, has put it, there are two or three taxi-meters running instead of one. After one lawyer, the solicitor, has involved himself in the case, become familiar with all the details, and developed a relationship with the client, the case is handed over to another lawyer, the barrister. He, in turn, has to spend costly time familiarizing himself with the case. The solicitor will have wasted more time in drawing up instructions to the barrister. If a conference with the client is held, both lawyers will be there, and when the case comes to court, the barrister, in most cases, has to be accompanied by the solicitor or his clerk.

At all these stages, the client (or, more usually, the taxpayer, through the legal aid scheme) is paying for two legal minds when, often, only one would do. The same may be true, though not as obviously, when the solicitor takes a case to a barrister not for advocacy, but for advice. In addition, the to-ing and fro-ing between the lawyers, and the need for two lawyers to find time for the case, increases the likelihood of delays. And, since success in a case depends to a large extent on the preparation that goes into it, the result is bound to be better if the person who has prepared the case and knows all the details presents it to the court as well. As Tony Holland, a Plymouth solicitor and Law Society Council member puts it:

> The old Marshall Hall type of advocacy has gone. If one goes into court and hears a civil dispute going on, the advocacy seems of a very dry and dull nature. It's the detailed knowledge of the case that counts. I think a solicitor can put across that detailed knowledge as easily as a barrister, particularly as he has been more in touch with the client and with the preparation of the case than the barrister has.

From the client's point of view, the system is often bewildering and illogical. After he has learned to trust his solicitor, he is told that the case in court is to be conducted by someone he has never met (and, again, may only meet on the morning of the court hearing) and who often appears to know less about the case than the solicitor does. It appears absurd to him that the person he wants to handle his case in court, who knows every detail of it, and in whom he has confidence, hands over to a stranger.

## Advantages

Defenders of the present system argue that doing away with the division will not necessarily lead to reduced duplication and lower costs. Even if there were only one class of lawyer, there would still be firms or individuals specializing in a particular kind of work, as in the United States. There would always be the need for one lawyer to refer to another for expert advice, and some degree of duplication would be inevitable. Moreover, a lawyer who is a specialist in his field is likely to save costs, because he can isolate the legal issues and solve them more quickly than the non-expert. In court he is less verbose, knows the points to concentrate on, and the trials in which he appears are likely to be shorter, cheaper and more successful. If all lawyers were allowed to be advocates in all courts, the general standard of advocacy would decline, and fewer would have the opportunity to become real experts, to the disadvantage of the client. It is also argued that there is an advantage in the barrister's detachment from the case. Richard Du Cann QC:

> When any advocate receives a set of papers, having no personal knowledge of the client involved, he can read that set of papers with his mind alive both to the facts and to the law which has to be applied to them, without being clouded by any feelings of personal allegiance or knowledge of the client at all. That means that he is not affected in any way in examining, as he has to, in a totally cold and clinical fashion, for the purpose of the presentation of the case before a court, all the issues which are going to arise.

The fear is that if there were a unified profession, the really good specialists now at the Bar would tend to be swallowed up by the big lawyers' firms, who could afford their services, and would no longer remain accessible to all. The small firms, especially those outside the big cities, would no longer have the benefit of being able to get advice from the large specialist pool that exists at present. They would either have to refer their clients to bigger firms – and possibly lose them for good – or try to deal with the matter themselves, with the possibility that their lack of experience in that area might deprive the client of the best advice.

## The Royal Commission on Legal Services

All these arguments were presented at great length to the Royal Commission on Legal Services, which reported in 1979. The bulk of the evidence on the structure of the profession submitted to the Commission favoured retaining the existing division. In particular, the Bar Council and the Law Society came down firmly in favour of the status quo, though the solicitors' body pressed for solicitors to be given greater rights of audience in the higher courts. Opposition to the present structure came from a minority of lawyers, especially those concerned with legal services to the poorer sections of the community.

The Royal Commission's conclusion was uncompromisingly against change, making few concessions to arguments the other way:

> We consider it likely that in a fused profession there would be an unacceptable reduction in the number and spread of the smaller firms of solicitors and an increase in the proportion of large city firms. This would accentuate the present uneven distribution of solicitors and reduce the choice and availability of legal services. We are satisfied that in the future there will be a greater need for specialization. Fusion would disperse the specialist service which is now provided by the Bar and we consider that this would operate against the public interest.

> In terms of cost . . . on balance, we believe that in small cases there might be some saving, but that in the larger cases this would not be so and the expense might be greater. With regard to the administration of justice, the weight of evidence is strongly to the effect that a two-branch profession is more likely than a fused one to ensure the high quality of advocacy which is indispensable, so long as our system remains in its present form, to secure the proper quality of justice. These considerations lead us to the unanimous conclusion that it is in the public interest for the legal profession to be organized, as at present, in two branches.

Since 1979, however, pressure for change has been building up, both within and outside the legal profession.

## Reform

While there is a growing body of support, particularly among younger lawyers, for a united legal profession, there seems little chance that anything so revolutionary will come about in the foreseeable future. However, many of the criticisms made about the existing structure of the legal profession could be met by introducing reforms which, while retaining the two-tier approach, would ensure that the 'specialist' branch genuinely lived up to that description.

Various proposals have been made over the years, and repeated in evidence to the Royal Commissions, for some kind of half-way house between the present system and total fusion of the profession. Broadly, such a compromise scheme – floated most recently by the Law Society – would provide all would-be lawyers with the same professional education and training. At first, after qualifying, all would practice as lawyers, doing more or less what solicitors do now. After a minimum period of general practice – say two or three years – they would be entitled to apply to become specialist lawyers, in advocacy or in a specific area of the law. To be admitted, they would have to satisfy some committee or professional body of their expertise and competence in the speciality in question. The division of the two branches would then be based genuinely on skill and knowledge and not on nomenclature and organization. But Robert Alexander, Chairman of the Bar for 1985-6, has come out strongly against the suggestion. 'In practice the proposal will present an overwhelming obstacle to those wanting to come to the Bar. It is a restriction on freedom of choice of profession.'

The Law Society is also pressing for greater rights of audience for solicitors in the higher courts. It recently supported an appeal from the High Court's refusal to allow Liberal MP Cyril Smith's solicitor to read out a libel apology in court. The appeal was turned down, but the High Court judges have since agreed to appear in the High Court to read out agreed statements and deal with other 'formal and unopposed' matters. The Bar is firmly opposed to any substantial extension of solicitors' rights of audience. Richard du Cann warns: 'If solicitors were given full rights of audience in all levels of court, they would cut the Bar to pieces in no more than three or four years.'

The Law Society argues that allowing solicitors a bigger role in the higher courts, even if this stops short of full rights of audience, would eliminate some of the drawbacks of the two-tier system. Sir David Napley, a past president of the Society:

> If a solicitor can find the time and has the skill to conduct a case in the magistrates' court, and that case is then committed to the higher court for trial because the prosecution ask for it, or the defendant wishes it, it does seem rather nonsensical to say that he's incapable of conducting that case in the higher court, which he would undoubtedly have conducted in the lower court. If he can do the one, he can do the other. And I would have thought he could probably do it as efficiently and with no greater and probably less expense.

Though the Royal Commission on Legal Services rejected the idea of giving solicitors wider rights of audience in the Crown Courts – for fear of harming the junior Bar – three members of the Commission dissented on this point. They favoured allowing solicitors to appear in the Crown Court in the less serious cases, cases where their clients are pleading guilty, appeals from the magistrates' courts, and committals for sentence by the magistrates. This would cut out the waste of time in simple cases in preparing briefs, holding conferences, and having two people in court when one would do.

# CHAPTER IV

# THE JUDGES

The English judge, much respected and much satirized, is to some people the awesome embodiment of wisdom, independence and impartiality in a free society. To others he is an elderly, remote, crusty figure wearing ridiculous fancy dress, speaking strange jargon and holding views more appropriate to the nineteenth century. He has been much represented and misrepresented in literature, and on film and television, with the result that the public has a somewhat bizarre idea of who he is and what he does.

The English judge emerges into the public gaze reluctantly to carry out as unobtrusively as he can the work which is required of him, and then he disappears back into the rarefied, cocooned atmosphere of the Inns of Court. Occasionally one or two judges become public figures because they are called on to perform extrajudicial functions of national importance – Lord Scarman's inquiries into the Brixton riots of 1981; Mr Justice Popplewell on safety at sports grounds following the Bradford fire tragedy in 1985; Lord Widgery on Londonderry's Bloody Sunday in 1972; Lord Wilberforce on the miners' pay dispute in 1972; and Lord Denning's report on the Profumo affair in 1963 are examples.

A few judges have delivered public lectures or written books. It was controversy over the most recent of Lord Denning's three lively works on the law that led to his retirement in 1982. In 1986 Judge James Pickles incurred official anger when he took part in radio programmes on prostitution and sentencing. But these are the exceptions. All but a few of our judges are virtually unknown to the public at large, even though they may have a reputation among lawyers. They may briefly stray into the limelight by passing a particularly stiff sentence or making a strong or a silly comment. But then they merge back into anonymity.

## The hierarchy

The first myth to be dispelled is that they always wear the full-bottomed wigs in which they are invariably pictured in the newspapers or in news films of the quaint ceremonies they attend. Full wigs are ceremonial only – in court they wear short versions which sit on the head rather than envelop it. And some of the most senior judges of all, the law lords, are not robed or wigged at all.

There are altogether nearly 500 full-time judges and as many again part-time. The most senior judge of all, and the head of the judiciary, is the Lord Chancellor.

> The law is the true embodiment
> Of everything that's excellent.
> It has no kind of fault or flaw
> And I, my lords, embody the law.
> Gilbert and Sullivan
> (*Iolanthe*)

His is a curious and unique position: he is a political appointee, given the job by the party in government and therefore losing it if his party loses the election. Usually he is himself a politician, although there is nothing to stop the Prime Minister choosing him from elsewhere. The one absolute requirement is that he must be a barrister.

The Lord Chancellor, currently Lord Hailsham of St Marylebone, has multiple duties. He is the government's chief spokesman on legal affairs in the House of Lords. He is a member of the cabinet, and Speaker of the House of Lords, sitting on the Woolsack in knee breeches and silk stockings. He is a key figure on State ceremonial occasions. He hands the Queen her speech on the opening of Parliament. He is also effectively the Minister of Justice; with the help of a large department he runs the administration of justice and the court system. He advises the Queen (for some ranks, through the Prime Minister), on what judges to appoint. He appoints magistrates. He can also preside over the law lords in the House of Lords. Most Lord Chancellors have been too busy with their many other duties but a few – including Lord Hailsham – have made a point of sitting with the law lords as often as possible.

The top professional judge is the Lord Chief Justice of England and Wales (Scotland and Northern Ireland have their own). Until recently there was a great deal of political patronage involved in achieving the office: anyone who had been Attorney-General had prior claim on the Lord Chief Justice's post. Today it goes with merit. The Lord Chief Justice can sit in any court but in practice he mainly presides over the Criminal Division of the Court of Appeal, where he is in a strong position to develop the law in the criminal field and lay down guidelines on sentencing policy: for instance when judges should not impose sentences of imprisonment or when a short sentence is appropriate.

The current holder of the office, Lord Lane, has been particularly active in urging courts to pass severe sentences of imprisonment on rapists and drug traffickers. The Lord Chief Justice is also the head of the Queen's Bench Division of the High Court and sometimes presides over the Divisional Court there.

The Master of the Rolls, next in the hierarchy, derives his title from his original duties as the keeper of national records. He sits in the civil branch of the Court of Appeal with two other appeal judges. Like the Lord Chief Justice on the criminal side, the Master of the Rolls has a great deal of influence over the development of the civil law. The judgments of Lord Denning, who held the office for twenty years until retiring in 1982, have profoundly affected virtually every field of the civil law.

After this, an oddity. The Lords of Appeal in Ordinary – the law lords – sit in the highest court in the land, the House of Lords. But although they are, in judicial terms, junior to the Lord Chief Justice and the Master of the Rolls, they can hear appeals from the decisions of those judges and their courts. The nine law lords are the Queen's appointment (on the advice of the Prime Minister). Two of them are usually Scottish judges; the others are normally promoted from the Court of Appeal. In addition, present and former Lord Chancellors are eligible to sit. The law lords are created life peers in their own right and in theory they are entitled to do everything that any other peer can do. By tradition, however, (occasionally broken) they participate only in debates on the law or the administration of justice.

Then come the judges of the Court of Appeal, the twenty-two Lords Justices who sit regularly in the civil division of the court, and some of them also in the criminal division. They also occasionally sit in the Queen's Bench Divisional Court. Appeal judges are promoted from the best of the High Court bench.

The next tier down are the High Court judges. In April 1986 there were seventy-four of them divided among the three divisions: forty-six in the Queen's Bench; twelve in Chancery; and sixteen in the Family Division. Judges are normally appointed to the High Court in their early fifties – usually twenty-five years or more since beginning their legal careers. They are picked from the most able of the senior barristers, almost invariably QCs. The limitation that High Court judges can only come from the ranks of barristers comes periodically under attack but shows no indications of being changed.

Circuit judges are next in line. There are 373 of them, serving as judges of the Crown Court hearing serious criminal cases (except the most grave, like murder, which circuit judges can try only by special consent of the Lord Chancellor), or in the county courts, dealing with minor civil cases. Unlike High Court judges, they receive no automatic knighthood, their pay is less than a good barrister can earn, and the cases they sit on are usually relatively straightforward, seldom offering the intellectual stimulation that judges of the High Court are accustomed to. Promotion from the circuit bench to the High Court is rare, so someone who applies for the office knows he is likely to remain there until reaching the pensionable age of seventy-two. Circuit judges tend to come mainly from the middle ranks of senior barristers. The really high-fliers, the most successful barristers, would hope to be invited on to the High Court bench and would not normally be interested in becoming circuit judges, for reasons of both finance and prestige. Most of those who do apply to be interviewed for the circuit bench are perfectly competent barristers who accept that they are not quite of High Court calibre and that they can get no further at the Bar. They plump for security and a pension. It is a source of concern, however, to the judiciary and the legal profession that, with such a large number of circuit judges needed and such a small pool to choose from, too many of them may be second-raters.

Solicitors are eligible for the circuit bench – the highest judicial notch to which they can aspire – but only thirty of the 373 are currently from their ranks.

The lowest judicial level is part-time. There are 586 recorders, of whom forty are solicitors, who sit for twenty or so days a year in the Crown Court. Appointment as a recorder gives a practising lawyer a taste of judging which he may later try to turn into a full-time occupation. It also gives the Lord Chancellor the opportunity to assess whether he has the ability to become a circuit or even a High Court judge.

A number of legally qualified officials below the level of judge are given certain judicial functions. County court registrars deal with many preliminary matters before trial, and play an important role in the courts dealing with divorce. Not only are they the filters through which all divorce applications must pass, but they also make most of the decisions about money and property. Registrars act as judges in small claims arbitrations, involving up to £500. Masters of the Queen's Bench Division and the Chancery Division of the High Court direct the conduct of cases up to the point where they go to trial. They give directions as to how a case should proceed to trial – for example, how many expert witnesses (such as doctors or engineers) each side should be allowed. In a case where there is really no defence to a claim for money owing, the Master can give judgment for the plaintiff at an early stage.

## How they are chosen

At the High Court level, becoming a judge is by invitation only and it is the Lord Chancellor who does the inviting. He chooses from a small and limited pool – senior barristers, almost always experienced

JUDGES

| Called | Court | Referred to as | Title | Addressed in Court | Retiring Age | Salary |
|--------|-------|----------------|-------|--------------------|--------------|--------|
| Lord of Appeal in Ordinary or law lord | House of Lords | Lord Wise | Peerage – Lord Wise | My Lord | 75 | £69,000 |
| Lord Justice of Appeal (appeal court judge) | Court of Appeal | Lord Justice Wise | Knighthood – Sir John Wise | My Lord | 75 | £66,000 |
| High Court Judge | High Court | Mr (or Mrs) Justice Wise | Knighthood – Sir John (or Dame Jean) Wise | My Lord My Lady | 75 | £60,000 |
| Circuit Judge | Crown Court or County Court | His (or Her) Honour Judge Wise QC (if a QC) | None | Your honour* | 72 | £40,000 |
| Recorder | Crown Court | Mr (or Mrs) Recorder Wise | None | Your honour | 72 | £191 per day |

*Judges of the Old Bailey, although strictly ordinary circuit judges, are addressed as 'My Lord'.

QCs. The only formal qualification is that the candidate should have been in practice for at least ten years. In former days, when the Bar was small, the Lord Chancellor knew all the able QCs personally and could assess which of them were good judge material. It is much more difficult now. He cannot know everyone; he has to base his appointments on advice from other judges, senior lawyers and reports from his departmental officials. It is largely an informal process. A judge who has been particularly impressed (or the opposite) with the performance of a barrister who has appeared before him might tell the Lord Chancellor so. Reputations spread. Little by little a dossier is built up. There will also be information about barristers from occasions when they have applied for lesser appointments; to become QCs or recorders, for instance. All is stored on what the Lord Chancellor's department refer to as the 'yellow sheets', which are in fact white. So by the time a senior barrister comes to be considered for the High Court bench, the Lord Chancellor has quite a lot of information on him or her which he can supplement by further enquiries from anyone who knows the candidate. And almost all candidates for the High Court bench have been recorders, so their judicial ability is not entirely unknown. Lord Elwyn-Jones, the Lord Chancellor in the 1974-9 Labour administration:

> You have his whole background, experience and what people have found him to be good at and not so good at – sometimes referees are inclined to turn every goose into a swan; sometimes they are alarmingly in the other direction.

There is finally a meeting between the Lord Chancellor and his senior judges. An informal short list is discussed. Usually one name emerges as the strongest, but the final decision is the Lord Chancellor's alone.

Such a system does, however, throw up some strange decisions. Some of the most brilliant barristers have never been offered high judicial appointment (for reasons which are never made public though they may have something to do with their personal life rather than their legal ability). At the same time there are some High Court judges of lesser ability. The system has recently come under some criticism, and calls have been made for a less secret, more accountable procedure.

There are some barristers who have been invited to become judges but have declined, mainly for financial reasons. For busy practising silks, becoming a High Court judge would entail a substantial drop in earnings. The gap is not as large now as it has been in the past – a High Court judge today receives £60,000 a year – and there is a large pension on retirement, but the money may still be an issue. There has been one example – Sir Henry Fisher, in 1970 – of a High Court judge who left the bench to take up a more lucrative appointment in the City, to the general disapproval of his fellow judges.

Promotion to the Court of Appeal and then to the House of Lords is in theory on the advice of the Prime Minister, but in practice these appointments too are the Lord Chancellor's. Once a judge has already been on the bench it is of course a far easier job to evaluate his ability for the highest judicial posts.

The junior judicial appointments – circuit judges and part-time recorders – don't require an invitation. Any reasonably senior barrister (not necessarily a QC) or solicitor can apply to the Lord Chancellor, and applicants are interviewed and assessed just as they would be for a job anywhere else. There is even a senior official of the Lord Chancellor's department whose job includes going around the courts 'talent spotting'. A solicitor, however, can only become a circuit judge after he has served three years as a recorder, and once a circuit judge he can go no further, however well he has performed and however high his reputation as a judge. There is a bar on solicitors becoming High Court judges, and of course this means that they cannot be appeal judges or law lords either.

This is absurd, according to the Law Society, which has been campaigning for a change in the law to allow solicitors to be eligible for the senior judiciary. At a time when good judges are in short supply it is illogical, they argue, to deny access to the High Court bench to able candidates who have already proved themselves as judges, merely because they belong to the wrong branch of the profession. But several parliamentary attempts to get the law changed have met the implacable opposition of the Lord Chancellor and the Bar. Is there a convincing reason for this reluctance, or is it, as solicitors believe, sheer protectionism on the part of the barristers' branch? A number of reasons have been advanced by the Lord Chancellor and his supporters. Lord Roskill, a law lord, gave as his ground in a House of Lords debate: 'I do not believe that anybody should be invited to preside in the High Court in civil jurisdiction unless that person has had not merely some but very considerable experience of advocacy in that court.'

Lord Edmund-Davies, a former law lord: 'The Bar is experienced in holding the client at a distance and I think that is ultimately better preparation for the bench.'

The Lord Chancellor, Lord Hailsham, is adamant that experience in practice in the High Court is an essential prerequisite of being a judge there. He points out that solicitors can always transfer to the other branch of the profession and become barristers – thus rendering them eligible to be High Court judges. The late Lord Widgery, who was Lord Chief Justice until 1980, started off as a solicitor. So did Sir Robert Megarry, Vice Chancellor (head of the Chancery Division). But in practice a solicitor would have to transfer early in his career to become senior enough at the Bar to be considered for the bench.

The Law Society comments:

> Many solicitors specialise in advocacy and spend most of their working life in court. Conversely, many barristers spend little time in court, and much more on paperwork. Many more clients are represented in court by solicitors than by barristers. Although through historical accident solicitors have no right to appear in the higher courts, they deal with the bulk of the preparation and carriage of High Court cases, and the solicitor whose practice involves High Court litigation needs a detailed knowledge of High Court procedure.

It argues that a number of High Court judges have been appointed who have had little experience at advocacy in the High Court, without finding it a handicap. Indeed, it is not unusual for barristers who have specialized all their lives in one area of the law to become judges dealing with a completely different field. Lord Elwyn-Jones, the former Lord Chancellor, admits that the Bar is opposed to allowing solicitors High Court parity because it is one of the attractions of the Bar that only barristers are eligible. Removing that 'perk' of the Bar would, he feels, undermine the divided profession. Faced with such strong feelings by those who hold the reins of power, there seems no immediate prospect of success for the campaign to put solicitors on the High Court bench.

There is more support in principle for another method of expanding the pool from which judges are chosen. Legal academics – professors and teachers of law – are often among the most knowledgeable experts in the country in their fields. It is true that they lack the relevant expertise to conduct full-scale trials with witnesses, and for this reason there are few who argue that they should be appointed to the High Court. But the appeal court and the House of Lords are forums in which they would revel. Argument on fine points of law precisely suits their training and experience. Lord Elwyn-Jones admits: 'We have been too apprehensive, too slow, in acknowledging the value that the academic could provide in the Court of Appeal.'

Most other countries have some form of career structure for judges but there is virtually no support for introducing a career judiciary in England. In France, for example, a young lawyer can choose while still in his twenties to enter the judiciary. He will be specially trained for it and start at the bottom with perhaps a minor post in a small town. In time he will expect to work his way up the ladder, just as in most other career structures.

English judges and lawyers believe that our system works

reasonably well and throws up judges of high quality and undoubted integrity. They argue that a career judiciary, and the jostling for advancement or particular postings that it would involve, would render judges more susceptible to state or other outside interference or persuasion. That may be an exaggeratedly critical view, but it would require a revolution in the legal system to change so drastically our mode of picking judges. There are no signs of either a need or a demand for such a change.

## Who are they?

Until relatively recently, twenty-five or so years ago, it was difficult even to consider becoming a barrister without some private funds or financial backing. Fewer grants were available from public funds to study law and it was much harder to make a living in the first few years of practice. A barrister often had to be supported financially not only for his period of study but perhaps for two or three years after being called to the Bar. The great legal aid explosion of the 1960s changed that and made it possible for young barristers to start earning very near the beginning of their careers; and the profusion of local authority grants (now under threat because of the economic climate) allowed more aspiring barristers to pursue their studies.

Our judges, however, are the products of the generation of barristers who, on the whole, had some source of private funds in their early years. Not surprisingly, the majority came from the comfortable middle and upper-middle classes, though there were some notable exceptions – Lord Denning's father was a draper.

It follows too that most of our present crop of judges, coming from relatively affluent families, have gone to public school and then to Oxford or Cambridge – in the region of 80 per cent of the senior judiciary. It's a proportion which has been approximately the same for the entire post-war period. There is a sprinkling of grammar school boys who won scholarships to an Oxbridge college (Lord Denning again), and public schoolboys who went to universities other than Oxbridge. One Court of Appeal judge sitting at present, Lord Justice Tasker Watkins VC, went to a Welsh grammar school and did not go on to university. He is very much an exception.

So the picture of our typical English judge emerges: middle class or above, public school, Oxbridge. And then, for many, war service. Only recently have we begun to get judges too young to have been in the war. Quite a few of today's judges have at one time flirted with a political career, mainly in the Conservative party. But even if they have not been Conservative in party loyalties, judges are almost invariably conservative with a small 'c'. Psychologists might say that young men who go into law are in any event showing a leaning towards things that are certain and slow to change, and a liking for the framework of rules. They would be firm supporters of the status quo, rather than radicals out to change it. Their careers as barristers would reinforce those predilections.

Most barristers who become judges – certainly those in London – have already spent twenty-five or even more years working, and often eating and drinking, in the rarefied and somewhat artificial atmosphere of the Inns of Court with their obscure and ancient customs and traditions. When they become judges the cocoon is tightened around them. The dignity of their office and the importance of being seen to be impartial and uncontroversial often demands that they distance themselves from their former habits and haunts, and even friends. The result can be an increasing remoteness from the mainstream of society. The longer they serve as judges, the more they may appear to be out of touch with the problems of the ordinary person. The charge is made against them that they live in an ivory tower, remote from the vicissitudes of most people's daily lives, unable from their lofty heights to appreciate the difficulties that lesser humans face. How true is that?

There is little doubt that in the past many judges believed themselves to be above the common herd. They were treated like royalty, especially when travelling round the country to sit in the peripatetic assize courts (a system now replaced by the permanent Crown Courts) and it is scarcely surprising that many of them started believing that they were akin to royalty. But things have changed. Judges today are convinced that they no longer inhabit that judicial ivory tower. Lord Edmund-Davies, a former law lord:

> Judges are human beings. They have families of their own, families have troubles, judges' families have troubles. Judges have friends who get into trouble. Judges have bills to pay, they have arrangements to make. They are not set apart, they are not cushioned. They are not surrounded by menials. They have to lead pretty normal lives off the bench.

Sir George Baker, the former president of the Family Division of the High Court:

> Normally this all starts on the basis that the judge doesn't go into the local pub, therefore he doesn't know what's happening. Don't you think that the judge will learn a great deal more about how people behave and what goes on from spending his time listening to the strange habits of husbands and wives than going nightly into his local pub? You learn quite as much from the process of hearing cases, coupled with your experience

at the Bar as you'd ever get from rubbing shoulders. The other thing I've always found is that whenever we get a bit remote or get a bit pompous there's one body that will always tell you, and that's your family.

It is true that judges today lead relatively normal lives when they are away from the bench and outside the Inns. They take public transport, drive cars, help with the washing up, go shopping, watch television and have children who play loud music. Few of them today have private incomes that enable them to live in luxury, though a judge's salary hardly keeps them in penury.

The English system of justice depends on respect for the judiciary, its independence and its integrity. To some extent that requires the judge to be a slightly awesome figure on a pedestal, and not one of the people. He must be Caesar's wife, above suspicion, careful and restrained in what he does and says.

## The role of the judge

The judge is a crucial figure in the English trial system, more so than in other countries. In the English process the result of a case turns very largely on what happens during the trial itself. In most other legal systems, much of the vital work is done before trial. There is much more documentary background material, and in a criminal case there has been a thorough investigation of the crime and the suspect long before an accused has to step into the dock.

The judge in an English trial plays many parts. First, he supervises the conduct of the trial. It is up to the parties and their lawyers to present their case, whether civil or criminal, but it is the judge who has to make sure that the rules are kept and that the trial flows as it should. A judge is like a football referee – if he is too lax, never blowing his whistle, the game gets out of control, the players take liberties and an unjust result may follow. If he is too strict and blows the whistle too often the game is ossified and the players get no chance to show their paces and use their skills – the game is equally distorted. A judge must put his firm stamp on the trial without taking over the proceedings.

Second, he is the sole arbiter of any legal issues that arise during the trial, in particular about the admissibility of evidence. This is especially important in criminal trials, where the case can hang on whether certain evidence can be put to the jury or not. There are numbers of other legal decisions which may need to be made in the course of a trial and which will affect it significantly.

Third, in civil cases the judge himself has to decide the result. Apart from rare libel cases, juries have in practice disappeared from civil trials. The judge is the sole arbiter. He not only determines who wins and who loses but also such issues as what damages to award, how to distribute money or property, which divorcing parent should have custody of the children, how an ambiguous rule should be interpreted, and so on through a wide range of decisions.

Fourth, when giving his judgment in a civil trial he has to interpret and clarify the law when there are gaps in it, or where it is unclear or ambiguous. Some would say that judges go further and actually make new law.

Fifth, in a criminal trial the judge has the important task of summing up to the jury. The verdict is the sole province of the jury, but it is the judge's duty both to guide them on the law and to summarize impartially the main factual points given by witnesses in evidence. Cases have been won or lost on a judge's summing-up. It has been known for a judge skilfully to nudge a jury towards his own conclusion, whether for conviction or acquittal. But this has to be done subtly. Juries resent being told what verdict to reach, and a crude summing-up may well be counter-productive.

Finally, and perhaps most important, a judge has to pass sentence on defendants who have pleaded guilty or who have been convicted by a jury. He is confined to the limits laid down by the law and within those limits there is often an unwritten informal tariff for particular kinds of offences. Judges also have guidance from the Court of Appeal about levels of sentencing. Nevertheless, sentencing is an awesome responsibility, especially where the decision is whether or not to send an offender to prison.

## Training

With all these different and difficult functions to perform it would be logical to assume that some training is given to judges before they are let loose in the courts. In fact very nearly the opposite is true.

It is one of the quirks of the system that a judge, once appointed, may be allocated to an area of the law about which he knows very little. It is quite common, for instance, for a barrister who has spent his entire professional career doing civil work to be called on to try serious criminal cases, or for someone whose practice was mainly in the criminal courts to have to decide divorce disputes. There is an unspoken, perhaps arrogant, assumption that anyone good enough to be appointed to the bench has the ability to turn his hand to any branch of the law. Sir Neville Faulks, a former High Court judge, admits in his autobiography that when he was appointed as a judge to try divorce cases – a subject about which he knew little since his practice at the Bar had been in libel – he spent the Christmas vacation 'reading very carefully *Rayden on Divorce.*' That, it seems, was his only training for the job to which he had been appointed. In practice the results of our rather haphazard system are mixed. Many a judge becomes known for his mastery of a field that he hardly touched as a barrister, but there are others who only feel at ease in the speciality they developed at the Bar.

Until recently the concept of giving judges any training to help them fulfil their new and perhaps unfamiliar duties was considered anathema, an insult to barristers. Not until 1963 was the first tentative step taken in the form of a one-day non-compulsory conference on sentencing. Judicial training (or judicial studies, as judges prefer to describe it) has expanded since then and it has become more formalized with the setting up of a Judicial Studies Board to run courses.

In 1972 a committee of the law reform body Justice recommended that there should be a three to six-month training period for all judges on their appointment. In 1978 an inter-departmental government committee, chaired by Lord Justice Bridge, suggested a period of one or two weeks, depending on whether the new appointee had experience in the criminal courts or not.

The present courses are less ambitious even than that modest proposal. There are two kinds of course, held in a comfortable though not luxurious country-house-turned-conference-centre in south west London. One is for beginners – mainly newly appointed recorders – and the other a refresher course for more experienced circuit judges.

The novices' course lasts three and a half days. They are given lectures by experienced judges about the duties they have to carry out in court, how to conduct a trial and the problems they may encounter. The main focus is on sentencing. They attend lectures by probation officers, social workers, prison officials, psychiatrists, and penologists as well as senior judges. These are designed to give trainee judges an idea of the interaction between offenders, their crimes and the options available to treat or punish them. They are fed with the latest important Court of Appeal decisions, prison statistics and information about trends in imprisonment and the alternatives to prison, like community service. They will all at some stage visit a prison and a youth custody institution.

Perhaps the most effective parts of the course are the sentencing exercises. The participants are given an outline of a crime committed, and information about the offender's history and background – the same information as judges in real trials would have. The facts are based on cases which have been before the Court of Appeal. The trainee judges discuss the cases among themselves, in small panels, and decide on the sentences they would pass. Their results are analysed and discussed by experienced judges and compared to the sentences the Court of Appeal imposed when it dealt with the real cases.

The refresher course for more experienced judges lasts the same amount of time, but is more advanced. The judges are assumed to know the basic principles, but they, too, have to be kept up to date with the latest case-law, and trends in sentencing policy and penology. There is much more discussion among themselves, and with senior judges, on issues actually confronting them in the courts, and fewer formal lectures. Sentencing is still likely to be the focus.

These courses are an improvement on what was being provided even a decade ago. In 1985 some 400 judges, recorders and assistant recorders attended a residential seminar. And the role of the Judicial Studies Board has been expanded to provide some training for judges sitting in the courts dealing with civil and family matters.

But even with these improvements, is the training provided anywhere near enough? Good advocates do not necessarily make good judges. The skills required of the two disciplines are not identical. Yet our system requires the transition from barrister to judge to be made with only minimal guidance. In most other walks of life new appointees to a job can usually gain their experience gradually, in a way which does no direct harm to anyone. Judges, in contrast, are obliged to cut their teeth immediately on human beings – whether litigants in civil cases or defendants in criminal trials. Three and a half days seems rather little preparation. Alex Lyon, a barrister and the Home Office minister who set up the committee whose proposals resulted in the Judicial Studies Board, is not alone in believing that it is not enough:

> It ought to be something of the order of three months, and it ought to involve visits to other countries and visits to all kinds of penal establishments and lectures from criminologists who have studied the effect of different kinds of penological treatment.
>
> The reason why it hasn't been extended is because of the resistance of advocates who have been at the Bar for many years, and the whole issue is so sensitive that we have to proceed very slowly. I think it must be made clear to people who may be very skilled in the art of advocacy that that doesn't necessarily fit them to be good judges.

Lord Devlin, in *The Judge* (Oxford University Press, 1979), takes an almost diametrically opposing view. He would prefer no training at all:

> There is no point in partial training; that would produce only a half-baked expert. If the judge is to be trained, he should be fully trained. He will then be an expert who holds views of his own. His decision will

cease to reflect the attitude of the ordinary man
applying an intelligent mind to technical questions and
will become itself the product of a technique.

He is particularly opposed to giving judges training in sentencing and
penology on the grounds that:

> . . . the judge is unlikely to make a good penologist,
> that the rehabilitation of the criminal depends less upon
> the judicial sentence than upon the manner of carrying it
> out, and that what is needed when giving the sentence is
> an impartial adjustment between the view of the expert
> on what fits the criminal and the view of the public on
> what fits the crime.

## The judge as lawmaker

Judges, according to the traditional litany, do not make law, they
only interpret existing law; they decide what the law already is. It is
Parliament's role to create new law, not the judiciary's. That may be
a perfectly reasonable theoretical position to hold and it is in keeping
with the constitutional division between the judiciary and the
legislature. It does not, however, conform to the facts. Judges can
and do make laws. It is in the nature of the British system of law.

Most countries in the world have legal codes. Every branch of the
law is governed by a code which lays down exactly what can and
cannot be done. It tries to cater for every contingency. When there is
a problem the judges turn to the code to see what it says. Of course
there are some gaps and some ambiguities and judges have to resolve
these, but their role is secondary.

Britain has no such comprehensive codes, and finding out what the
law is can be rather more complicated. There are two main sources
of law and the judges play a central role in both. The first is statute
law – Acts of Parliament (from which may stem a whole range of
lesser laws passed by other bodies, like local authorities). The United
Kingdom Parliament is sovereign; it can pass any law on any subject.
But many of these laws are imperfectly drafted. They are not always
clear. The intention behind them can be obscure. There are gaps,
both deliberate and accidental. Sometimes two interpretations are
possible. When there is room for doubt about what an Act of
Parliament actually means, it is the judges' job to clarify it. Their
interpretation can have the most dramatic results, not just for the
people involved in the case itself but for millions of other people in a
similar position.

The common law of England, the other main source of law, will not be found in any Act of Parliament. It has developed over the centuries through the decisions of judges in particular cases that have come before them, in areas where there is no statute. These decisions are not taken haphazardly – the law would be chaotic and uncertain if it were left entirely to each judge to decide the case according to his whim. So there has grown up the doctrine of precedent based on the understandable assumption that the higher courts, made up of the most senior judges, know better than the lower judiciary. There are courts whose decisions must be followed by lower ranking courts. Decisions of the House of Lords, the highest court, are binding on all the other courts below it, and even on itself unless the law lords are convinced that a previous decision was wrong. If the House of Lords has not ruled on a particular point, then it is the Court of Appeal's decisions that are binding on the lower courts. A High Court judge, for instance, must follow them, even if he thinks they are wrong.

Lord Edmund-Davies explains how judges approach their role as interpreters of the law:

> If it's a matter of construing a statute, his duty is to give every word of the statute its proper meaning as he judges it, regardless of the consequences. Obviously if an approach of that kind leads to a manifestly undesirable – by that I mean unjust – result, he will struggle his best, being human, to see whether another interpretation is consistent with the statute. But if it is not, his duty is quite clear: he must give the interpretation which he finds forced upon him, express his deep regret at the conclusion he is driven to and express the fervent hope that the legislature will do something about it.

Curiously, and illogically, judges are allowed to take into account the purpose of a statute to help them in interpreting it, but they are not allowed to find out that purpose from Hansard, the report of Parliament, which would usually be the best source of what the statute was intended to do. Lord Elwyn-Jones:

> He does his best first of all to apply the language that Parliament has introduced into the Act – that's his primary task. He can't bend the law as he thinks fit to meet a given case. He has got to apply the law as he finds it. Otherwise the law will reach such a state of uncertainty that no citizen knows where he stands. And that's why the law has to be clear and plain as far as possible, and the judge's task is above all to apply the law as he finds it.
>
> If the law itself is ambiguous or its intent is not wholly

clear, he should do his best to apply the law to deal with the mischief, on the criminal side, that the Act of Parliament is intended to deal with, or on the civil side, the purpose for which the legislation is intended. He has to do his best to the limits of not doing violence to the language of the Act.

What can a judge do if the precedent he is bound to follow achieves injustice? Lord Edmund-Davies:

> Justice that pays no regard to precedent can be positively injustice. Precedents can be grossly irritating and confining when they exist and prevent you from going the way you would prefer to go. But I do not agree that justice can always be arrived at by ignoring precedent. If you are not bound, of course, it's another matter. Do the just thing as you see it. But sometimes that is quite impossible.
>
> I would struggle might and main to differentiate between a line of existing cases and the instant case in order to arrive at a just conclusion. But if there is really no substantial difference between the case I have in hand and earlier cases I cannot, consistent with my duty, forget those earlier cases, although I might be most unhappy in coming to the conclusion I find myself driven to arrive at. And leave it to Parliament. Because I think that if you do not adopt that approach, chaos can arrive, and chaos and justice in my view are ill neighbours.

Lord Denning, who retired as Master of the Rolls in 1982, argued passionately that judges were too conservative in interpreting the law to achieve the just result. His philosophy is summed up in his book *The Discipline of Law* (Butterworths, 1979):

> Let it not be thought from this discourse that I am against the doctrine of precedent. I am not. All that I am against is its too rigid application, a rigidity which insists that a bad precedent must necessarily be followed. I would treat it as you would a path through the woods: you must follow it certainly so as to reach your end, but you must not let the path become too overgrown, you must cut out the dead wood and trim off the side branches, else you will find yourself lost in thickets and brambles. My plea is simply to keep the path of justice clear of obstructions which would impede it.

Lord Denning's scant regard for precedents which stood in the way of what he believed to be justice attracted much criticism from many of his legal and judicial colleagues. A goodly proportion of his decisions in the Court of Appeal were overturned by the House of Lords. But his insistence on doing justice even by straining the law also gained him respect and admiration from millions of people outside the legal world.

But did he take the function of a judge too far? Lord Devlin, one of the top legal minds of recent times, is one of the main proponents of judicial conservatism. Judges, he argues in *The Judge,* are not fitted for a creative, dynamic law-making role, nor is it desirable that they should be in the forefront of making law. Nor should they become social reformers, or become professionally concerned with social justice: 'It might be dangerous if they were. They might not administer the law fairly if they were constantly questioning its justice or agitating their minds about its improvement.'

But if judges should not see themselves as social reformers, they must inevitably be aware of the social and possibly the political background of the cases that come before them. Judges too have private opinions and prejudices. Professor John Griffith suggests, in *The Politics of the Judiciary* (Fontana, 1985), that the higher judiciary:

> . . . have by their education and training and the pursuit of their profession as barristers, acquired a strikingly homogeneous collection of attitudes, beliefs and principles, which to them represents the public interest. They do not always express it as such. But it is the lodestar by which they navigate.

In theory, judges must try to put aside not only their own views but also what they know or suspect might be the wider practical consequences of their decisions. Professor Griffith doesn't believe that complete neutrality can be achieved in practice. Judges, he argues, by their own inclinations and because of the status of the judiciary as part of the authority within the state, will tend to make conservative decisions which support the existing order as they see it:

> It is demonstrable that on every major social issue which has come before the courts during the last thirty years – concerning industrial relations, political protest, race relations, governmental secrecy, police powers, moral behaviour – the judges have supported the conventional, established and settled interests. And they have reacted strongly against challenges to those interests.

Judges vigorously deny that they come to decisions on the basis of political considerations. In any event, they argue, is it not in the public interest that judges should be conservative, favour the status quo, and be suspicious of flash new legal theories and arguments based on a particular view of social justice? Lord Devlin:

> Law is the gatekeeper of the status quo. There is always a host of new ideas galloping around the outskirts of a society's thought. All of them seek admission but each must first win its spurs; the law at first resists, but will submit to a conqueror and become his servant. (*The Judge*).

The debate continues. If there is a trend to be discerned it is that judges have become more obviously aware of the social, political and administrative circumstances that form the backdrop to any case before them. They are also much more conscious of public opinion on particular issues and although they must not formulate their decisions to conform to public opinion, it can, judges admit, have some effect on their minds. Judges are perhaps more adventurous than they used to be, not as awed by precedent or as timid in making known their views on the law.

At the same time Parliament is becoming far more active in passing new laws. The sheer amount of legislation pouring through Westminster is having its effect on the courts. Statute law is coming to dominate the common law. This is partly deliberate – it is government policy, aided and abetted by the Law Commission, the government's law reform advisory arm, to try to codify the whole of the criminal law and some areas of the civil law – and partly a sign of the times that requires everything to be set down on paper. The judges, however, will continue to play a crucial part. Their role is not diminishing. If anything they are becoming even more essential.

# CHAPTER V

# THE MAGISTRATES

If the English system of criminal justice had to depend on our professional judges, it would break down immediately. There are just too few judges to cope – fewer than 500 full-time ones. It doesn't collapse, because the judiciary is backed by about 27,000 magistrates who, astonishingly, are unpaid, part-time and amateur. The magistrates (or justices of the peace, or JPs) are not just important cogs: they are the mainstay of the criminal justice system. They deal with no less than 98 per cent of all criminal cases. Two and a half million people pass through their courts every year. Admittedly, most of them are charged with trivial crimes, for instance minor traffic offences, but in 1984 more than 15,000 offenders were sent to prison by magistrates.

This great power over the lives of others is concentrated in the hands of people who are chosen in secret, are given only minimal training to enable them to do their job, and work on a voluntary basis. Certainly if a legal system were to be created from scratch, no one would think of giving work of such importance to non-professionals. Like so many other British institutions, the lay magistracy grew and developed over the centuries until it became so vital a part of our legal system that it is now inconceivable to think seriously of changing it.

The first Justices or Keepers of the Peace were appointed as early as 1195 by Richard I, the Lionheart, and for the next century and a half they acted as a sort of primitive police force. During the fourteenth century, and especially during the economic and social chaos that followed the Black Death, they became in effect the local government, and they were also given the powers to dispense summary justice. A statute of 1361 provides:

> In every county of England shall be assigned for the keeping of the peace one lord and with him three or four of the most worthy in the county, with some learned in the law, and they shall have the power to restrain the offenders . . . and to pursue, arrest, take and chastise them according to their trespass and offence.

They kept all their roles for five centuries, though the distinction between their policing and judicial functions was not always clearly defined. During the great reform movements of the mid-nineteenth century they lost first their police role to the embryo modern police force, and then their administrative role to the emerging local councils, but they retained their judicial duties.

In London, the lay magistracy went through a period of great and justified unpopularity during the eighteenth century. Magistrates had a financial stake in the booty found on captured criminals. They were corrupt. Justice could be bought. So appalling had the reputation and standing of London's 'poor courts' become that the government passed a law allowing the appointment of lawyers as full-time stipendiary (paid) magistrates. Henry Fielding, the author of *Tom Jones*, was among the first of these stipendiaries, who worked in a house in Bow Street, forerunner of the famous Bow Street Magistrates' Court, the senior magistrates' court in the country. Fielding was succeeded by his brother, the blind John Fielding, whose Bow Street Runners were the direct precursors of today's Metropolitan Police Force.

The introduction of the few stipendiaries made little inroad into the system of lay justices, which eventually recovered its reputation and continued to expand. It was not until the 1920s and '30s, however, when motoring offences started to bring the articulate middle classes into the justices' courts, that reforms began to be made which laid the foundations of the modern magistrates' courts. The system as it is today is the result of a post-war reform following the recommendations of a Royal Commission in 1948.

## How are they chosen?

A magistrate need have no formal qualifications. But there are some disqualifications – those not eligible include bankrupts, those with a conviction for serious crime, members of the armed forces, the police, traffic wardens, or anyone with impaired hearing or sight or other serious infirmity. MPs, Parliamentary candidates or full-time election agents cannot be JPs in their own constituences, though they can sit in others. 'Any person whose office or whose work would conflict or be incompatible with the duties of a magistrate' cannot be one, nor can close relatives of justices on the same bench.

Very little, however, is said about the positive qualities magistrates need to have. The official booklet on the appointment of JPs describes them shortly:

> The first and much the most important consideration in selecting Justices of the Peace is that they should be personally suitable in character, integrity and understanding for the important work which they have

to perform, and that they should be generally recognized as such by those among whom they live and work. Under no circumstances will the Lord Chancellor appoint anyone as a reward for past services of any kind.

The process of choosing magistrates is subtle and secretive. There are no competitive examinations, and the only public trawl is through the occasional newspaper advertisement. Constitutionally, the appointment of magistrates lies with the Lord Chancellor, but in practice the task of choosing suitable candidates has been given to advisory committees all around the country. These committees recommend names to the Lord Chancellor, who then formally appoints them. He has the power to reject the committee's recommendation or to appoint someone without their advice, but he rarely does either. The Lord Chancellor relies heavily on the advisory committees, who have the local knowledge and the opportunity to assess and interview those they think might have the qualities to sit on the bench.

There are about 100 advisory committees in England and Wales, each with responsibility for a specified area. The curious and controversial fact about these committees is that, with a very few exceptions, they do not publicly reveal the identity of their members, except for the secretaries (so that those putting a name forward know to whom to write). The reason given for this secrecy is to prevent committee members being lobbied. Sir Thomas Skyrme, who was for thirty years the official in the Lord Chancellor's department responsible for advisory committees, explains in *The Changing Imge of the Magistracy* (Macmillan, 1979):

> Most committees prefer anonymity because it protects their members from being lobbied. There have been occasions when members whose identity had become known were subjected to such undue influence and persistent importuning that they felt obliged to resign. Experience also showed that disclosure of the composition of a committee led to dissatisfaction among sections of the local population, who complained that they were not represented; yet if members of every section were included the committee would become unmanageable.

What is known about the composition of the advisory committees is that they generally consist of about twelve members (and there may be smaller sub-committees). It is a rule that a committee should include at least one member from each of the main political parties and some members who are politically independent. Otherwise there are no hard and fast criteria. The Lord Chancellor appoints people to the committee whom he believes are in touch with local affairs and active and established in the local community, and therefore in a good position to assess who would make a good JP.

Anyone is entitled to recommend anyone else to the advisory committee as a suitable candidate for the magistracy. In theory, a person can recommend himself or herself, but the majority of candidates are approached by the committee because they are known personally or by reputation to committee members. This raises the criticism that advisory committees, being largely middle and upper class and 'establishment', tend to choose as magistrates others of their kind, and that the advisory committee system therefore produces a largely self-perpetuating oligarchy from which, in general the ethnic minorities and working-class people are excluded. In 1973, for instance, a survey of Rochdale magistrates showed that twenty-nine out of the forty-three were Freemasons or members of the Rotary Club and that not a single one was Roman Catholic. Even then such an imbalance was untypical. Today it would certainly be contrary to the Lord Chancellor's department's policy – a 'jobs for the boys' approach would be severely frowned on officially. But it may be to some extent inevitable under the present selection system.

## Who are they?

Sir Thomas Skyrme claims:

> The system of lay justices reflects, through citizen participation, the traditional English involvement of the layman in the administration of justice. It enables the citizen to see that the law is his law, administered by men and women like himself, and that it is not the esoteric preserve of the lawyers. (*The Changing Image of the Magistracy*).

But the statistics show that around 84 per cent of magistrates belong to what would loosely be called the professional or managerial classes – in other words, the middle classes and above. Only 16 per cent come from the skilled or semi-skilled working class and trade union officials. The Lord Chancellor's department admits that one of the reasons there are not more working-class magistrates is because they don't come to the attention of the advisory committees in the same way as middle-class candidates do – they don't move in the same circles or belong to the same clubs. Those that become active in politics or trade union affairs might be recommended by their party or union officials, but others may just never have their ability noticed and brought to the attention of the advisory committee.

There are other reasons too. Working-class people are often loath to allow their names to be put forward, either through lack of interest or because they fear that their job or promotion prospects might be endangered by their absences from work; or even on the ground that becoming a JP would cause tensions with their workmates and colleagues. These factors are exacerbated during a period of recession and high unemployment. If a working JP loses his job, he might find it difficult to get another once a prospective employer finds out he has to have a day off every fortnight. This is not confined to working-class wage-earners. In 1982, an applicant for the headmastership of a school was told that he could have the job on condition that he gave up his magisterial duties. Magistrates may also have to sacrifice part of their pay: the loss of earnings allowance (£24 a full day; £12 if they just sit for a morning) is less than most skilled workers earn. There should be no difficulty, in theory, about absences from work. Under the law, employers cannot object to their workers' taking time off to sit on the bench. In practice, however, there are many subtle ways in which an employer can make his displeasure known.

Whatever the reasons for the disproportionate social balance, it has led to comments that there is too much of a gap between the mainly middle-class, white, comfortably-off magistrates and the typical defendants who appear before them. Magistrates, it is suggested, cannot really understand the problems of the kind of people they try. If true, this would seem to contradict one of the aims of the system of lay justices.

More recently, concern has been expressed about the low proportion of magistrates from the ethnic communities, especially West Indian, Indian and Pakistani. Exact figures are not kept, but it is known that there were fewer than 100 black or Asian JPs in the 1970s, a proportion of less than half a per cent, at a time when the proportion in the population generally, especially in some large urban centres, was several times that, and perhaps more important, when there has been an increase in the number of black defendants before the courts. The figure is probably above 200 now, still vastly under-representative. Sir Thomas Skyrme explains:

> One must remember that the whole phenomenon of large populations from these ethnic groups is fairly recent. You can't just take anybody as soon as he arrives in this country and put him or her on the bench. They've got to have had a good deal of experience of this country because they're not only concerned with the affairs of their own people from their own country, they have got to sit in judgment over the white indigenous population and others, and they've got to know all the problems which affect people in this country. And therefore,

before they're really able to do that, they've got to have lived here long enough to have gained experience of the way of life of people here, of the population, of their customs and their problems and so on, and this has taken time.

We're getting on to the second generation, people who have been born here and have grown up here and with that, the numbers are increasing.

The attempt to get more women on the bench has been more successful – partly because many more women than men are not in full-time work – and the ratio of men to women is now about 3 to 2 (16,000 men and 11,000 women approximately).

A fine balance has to be drawn. It is crucial to our system of justice to have magistrates who are good at what they do. But it is equally important for the public at large and for defendants in particular to feel that they are not too remote from those who sit in judgment on them. If it were widely thought that magistrates were too unrepresentative of the society which they served, their reputation would suffer and public respect for our system of justice would be damaged.

In 1947 about a quarter of sitting magistrates were over seventy, and there were even some over ninety. Only 12 per cent were under fifty and only just over one out of every hundred were under forty. That pattern has changed considerably. Now seventy is the compulsory retiring age and it is a rule that no one should be appointed for the first time above the age of sixty (in practice, fifty-five). Today the average age of JPs is under fifty (exact statistics are not kept), thousands are under forty, and there are now even some magistrates in their twenties. But the average age of benches is still not as low as the Lord Chancellor's department would like, in spite of efforts made to recruit younger JPs – in their thirties. For one thing, men and women with young families find it more difficult to devote their time to magisterial duties. Moreover, it is precisely at that period of their working lives that ambitious and able people are actively pursuing their careers. Although there is a certain prestige in becoming a magistrate, many employees feel that their regular absences would inevitably affect their chances of promotion. Self-employed, professional and business men and women simply cannot spare the time and loss of income which becoming a magistrate might entail. Women who do not work full-time have been a traditional source for recruitment, but the pattern of the working husband and the non- or only part-working wife is itself breaking down. Getting young magistrates is likely to continue to be a problem, but at least the public image of a magistrate of not so long ago – rubicund, elderly local squire, or crusty retired colonel – is now very far from the truth.

## Training

Only since 1966 have new justices of the peace received any compulsory training at all. Even now what they get is very basic – enough to acquaint them with their duties and tell them a little about the decisions they will be making. It is certainly not aimed at making them legal experts. The expertise is provided by the justices' clerk.

Training for new JPs is divided into two parts. After they are appointed but before sitting for the first time, they are given four lectures of about two hours each on their duties and their jurisdiction, the practice and procedure of the court and methods of punishment and treatment. They also have to sit as observers in a few different courts to see them in action from the public's point of view. After that first part of training (which can take as little as fourteen hours), magistrates are entitled to sit on the bench, though in the company of far more experienced colleagues.

The second stage of training is held within twelve months. It is a more intensive course of about ten sessions in which magistrates discuss with their clerk the laws they have to apply in more detail, and participate in practical exercises on bail and sentencing, two of the most important decisions they have to make. In the sentencing exercise, conducted by the justices' clerk, the magistrates are given the backgrounds of convicted offenders and details of their crimes, and have to decide how to deal with them. They discuss the options, which include an absolute or conditional discharge, a fine, probation, community service, imprisonment. They also attend lectures by probation officers and other officials involved with the courts. In addition, they visit a prison, a youth custody centre, and see various forms of non-custodial schemes in action.

All this still does not add up to anything remotely close to a professional education. How can we allow such thinly trained people to take on such awesome responsibilities? The answer is three-fold. First, the people chosen are supposed to have exhibited already in their careers, or in work for their community, or in some other way, the kind of qualities that will make them capable of judging and sentencing others with commonsense and understanding. Second, they can acquire experience gradually, from sitting on the bench under the guidance of more senior JPs. They also have to attend annual brush-up courses. Third, they lean heavily on their justices' clerk to fill the gaps in their legal knowledge or experience.

## The Justices' Clerk

Our system of lay magistrates relies on professional back-up and administration. Someone has to run the shop, and it cannot be the amateurs. The justices' clerk – who has to be a barrister or solicitor – is the pivotal figure of the magistrates' court. He is its chief executive and administrator, responsible for making the courts run efficiently, the legal adviser and mentor to the magistrates, and their instructor, responsible for training them in their duties. But during the trial itself, his functions are circumscribed. Brian Harris QC, a former President of the Justices' Clerks Society, explains:

> When he gives his advice it's very important that he shouldn't in any way express a view as to the facts of the case, because that's not for him. He mustn't give his assessment, even if he may have made one, on the credibility of the witnesses. He mustn't, even by the raising of an eyebrow, express disbelief in certain testimony. All that is for the magistrates to decide. But he must ensure that they understand the principles upon which they decide, the admissibility of the evidence upon which they are called to act. In other words, that they are in full possession of the proper legal principles upon which to act.

There are 324 justices' clerks in England and Wales, but they have assistants, some of whom are also legally qualified. Eventually the aim is that all justices' clerks' assistants (or magisterial officers) should have some legal qualifications, though not necessarily as a barrister or solicitor.

The justices' clerk has also been given some quasi-judicial functions himself – issuing summonses and granting legal aid, for instance – and the Justices' Clerks Society has been campaigning for clerks to be given wider discretion to make certain decisions. It seems a faintly absurd consequence of the system that the person with the knowledge and legal experience – the justices' clerk – has only limited powers, whereas those who have the power – the magistrates – often cannot exercise it without calling in the clerk's help.

## The stipendiary magistrate

The lay magistracy numbered 27,000 in 1986. The stipendiaries – paid, full-time, legally qualified magistrates – number only sixty – forty-eight in London, the others dotted around some of the bigger urban centres. Originally appointed when the reputation of the lay magistracy was at a low ebb, the few stipendiaries have remained part of the system. For the most part, stipendiary and lay justices co-exist reasonably happily together, even when they inhabit the same court. There has never been any serious call either to replace lay with paid justices altogether or to do away with the stipendiaries. Nevertheless, it is widely accepted that stipendiaries dispense a different kind of justice from that meted out by part-time justices, though there is no agreement as to which is preferable: some say that the full-time 'stipe' quickly becomes case-hardened and strict, others say that he is much more professional and fair.

The top stipendiary magistrate is the Chief Metropolitan Magistrate, who sits at Bow Street Magistrates' Court. All extradition requests have to be considered by him or another Bow Street magistrate. Perhaps almost as well known is Marlborough Street Court, where most offences committed in the West End first come. At one end of the scale there is the daily procession of drunks, prostitutes and illegal street sellers. But there are also the famous names, involved perhaps in a fracas in a nightclub, and there are the shoplifters from all over the world, drawn to Oxford Street's golden mile.

## The future of the lay magistracy

The lay magistrates' system in England and Wales is undoubtedly very quick, very cheap and pretty rough and ready. It is also reasonably efficient. Four main criticisms are made against it.

First, it is said that magistrates are too hasty and crude in the justice they dispense, that a magistrates' court can sometimes be confusing for the people who pass through it, and that injustice can result. Pat Carlen, author of *Magistrates' Justice* (Martin Robertson, 1976), a survey of what happens to defendants in the magistrates' courts, describes what she found:

> It's quite common to call the magistrates' courts 'assembly line justice' or a 'sausage machine'. Defendants are pushed through very rapidly. I've seen eight drunks going through the court in two minutes. There isn't time to explain. Most of the defendants plead guilty. The clerk doesn't explain the meaning of questions so the defendants tend to just go along and agree, and often if the defendant doesn't answer, the clerk or the magistrate fills in the answer for him.
>
> The organisation of the court and the layout of the courtroom and the legal rules themselves all operate to exclude the defendant from the trial. To the average defendant the court appearance is extremely disappointing. When they get into court I think that most of them are amazed to find that they are the people who are furthest away from the magistrate, and that they are pushed along by the police, told when to stand up and when to sit down and that they are given no information. Many of them don't know who is the magistrate and who is the clerk, and gradually you see them tend to give up, not trying to say anything at all.

One of the solutions is to provide more information to defendants who come before the magistrates. Another is for the magistrates themselves, and their clerks, to be a little more conscious of the difficulties faced by defendants in court for the first time, and a little more patient with them. Admittedly, the scene Pat Carlen describes is in a busy urban court; courts in the country, and their magistrates, tend to be less daunting.

The second criticism is that magistrates tend to be prosecution-minded and too inclined to believe police witnesses automatically. A London solicitor summarises what many who specialize in the criminal field feel – he points out that, especially in country areas:

> . . . the same magistrates see the same police giving evidence all the time and it follows therefore that they establish some sort of rapport, some sort of relationship with those individual police officers. That, coupled with the fact that the magistrates tend to come from an area of the community which does not have adverse contact with the police generally, tends to result in the lay magistrates accepting without question the evidence of police.

Another solicitor puts it this way:

> Clearly the way in which they look upon the police is governed and conditioned by their own social background and how they perceive the police to be. They are naive in many ways when they consider whether or not a police officer is telling the truth, as the view that they tend to hold is that a police officer has no reason not to tell the truth. They do not give the impression of looking on evidence presented by a police officer and a defendant in a completely even-handed manner.

Sir Thomas Skyrme agrees that magistrates used to accept police evidence too readily in the past, but no longer:

> I think it has changed enormously as a result of training. One of the very first principles which is instilled in the minds of any new justices is that in this country everybody is innocent until proved guilty, and that the onus of proving guilt rests on the prosecution and unless the prosecution have proved it to the satisfaction of the court, then the court must acquit and regard the accused as innocent.

The third main criticism is that there is too much of a social barrier between the magistrates and the defendants. If that is so and if indeed injustice does result, it is a difficult matter to put right. The Lord Chancellor's department tries hard to get a wider social and ethnic spread of justices. That it has not sufficiently succeeded is largely due to complex factors outside its control.

The fourth criticism is that magistrates are conviction-minded. It is widely believed that an accused has a better chance of being acquitted by a jury than by magistrates. Statistics are difficult to come by, partly because it was recently discovered that the magistrates' court figures which formed the basis of comparisons had been wrongly collated. Research using correct data is limited to relatively small samples, but the results suggest that magistrates convict up to 75 per cent of defendants who plead not guilty before them, whereas the acquittal rate for defendants choosing trial by jury is about 50 per cent. Magistrates argue that this merely shows that they are less often taken in than juries, not that they are convicting many innocent defendants. But some critics believe that wrongful, as well as justified, convictions are more likely in magistrates' trials, mainly because magistrates' courts do not have the time to be as thorough.

Whatever its faults, most lawyers and others who have come into contact with the system believe that on the whole it works. Magistrates deliver justice enormously cheaply (proportionately, England has easily the lowest bill for judicial services of any developed country), and relatively speedily and efficiently. The lay magistracy does the job asked of it and it offers good value for money. No serious contenders have been proposed to replace it and it is likely to remain the cornerstone of our justice system for the foreseeable future.

# CHAPTER VI

# THE CRIMINAL
# PROCESS

John Smith is thirty-six, married with two children. He is a contract furniture salesman, a job that involves him in 40,000 miles of driving a year. One November morning he leaves his house later than his usual eight o'clock. He is in a hurry. A few minutes later he is driving down Laurel Avenue and about to overtake a blue builders' van. Suddenly the van swerves out into the middle of the road and then turns sharply left into Cornwallis Road, which forms a T-junction with Laurel Avenue. Smith is forced out into the middle of the road. He cannot see whether anything is coming out of Cornwallis Road. As he passes the blue van, a motor cycle suddenly appears in front of him. He takes what emergency action he can, and swerves out even further to the wrong side of the road. Somehow he misses the motor bike.

Anne Jones, aged twenty-five, has just taken her five-year-old daughter Katy to school, and is on her way to work. She is about to cross Laurel Avenue; she looks to both sides and steps off the kerb. Suddenly she becomes aware of a car bearing down on her at speed on the wrong side of the road. A split second later it hits her. She is lifted on to the bonnet and then thrown down into the gutter. She lies there, unconscious.

John Smith stops his car and rushes up to try to help. Eventually an ambulance is called to give Anne Jones medical attention. A policeman appears on the scene, and starts asking Smith and a nearby eye-witness about the accident.

From that moment on, John Smith – like more than two million other people every year – finds himself embroiled in the criminal process. For the majority the involvement is slight. They may not even have to go to court. Most of those accused of minor traffic offences, for instance, can usually plead guilty by letter or, if they have to attend court, the case will be over quickly, and the sentence will be a small fine. What often matters is not the sentence itself, but the fact that it results in a criminal record that can have grave consequences for a person's career and reputation. The tiniest theft is still an offence of dishonesty, liable to bar the way to certain jobs. And even relatively trivial motoring offences can be significant if the driver needs his car for his livelihood. Perhaps even more important to some people is their standing among their friends, neighbours and colleagues. A moment's lapse – whether loss of temper or yielding to temptation – resulting in a minor criminal charge can destroy a person's reputation and status where it counts most, in his community. So it is not just those accused of serious crime and facing possible imprisonment for whom the process of criminal justice is desperately frightening. It is a chastening experience for all but the most hardened offenders.

## THE FIRST STEPS

For John Smith the first formal step on the long and complex road to trial starts when the policeman called to the scene of the accident makes up his mind that Smith has probably committed an offence – either careless or reckless driving. The moment he comes to this conclusion he has to administer the famous caution: 'You are not obliged to say anything, unless you wish to do so, but what you say may be put into writing and given in evidence.'

This does not mean that Smith will necessarily be prosecuted – sometimes the police will decide that there is not enough evidence. But the caution puts Smith on warning that he will probably face a charge. He decides to remain silent.

There are more dramatic ways of coming into conflict with the law, by being arrested for instance. Arrest is the process of placing someone suspected of a crime in legal custody. It can be done with the help of a warrant of arrest – a document signed by a magistrate when he has been persuaded by the police that there is enough evidence against the person involved. Nowadays warrants are not often used to arrest suspected criminals, though they continue to be issued when defendants out on bail fail to turn up.

Mostly, arrests are carried out without a warrant, by a policeman who reasonably suspects that a person has committed, is committing, or is about to commit a serious offence, one punishable by at least five years imprisonment – the technical term is 'arrestable offence'. Then there are various specific laws allowing a policeman to arrest without warrant for some lesser offences. He must caution anyone he arrests, telling him what crime he is suspected of, and that he has the right to remain silent. In addition, any individual has the right to arrest someone committing an arrestable offence. This is what is known as making a citizen's arrest.

### The decision to prosecute

The year 1986 has seen one of the most fundamental reforms in the history of the English criminal justice system. Until then, the decision to prosecute was largely in the hands of the police. But that system was haphazard and inconsistent. The forty-three police areas in England and Wales each had its own way of deciding on prosecution. Policies and arrangements differed.

An even more basic objection was identified by the Royal Commission on Criminal Procedure. It was not in the public interest or in the interests of justice, the Commission felt, that the very people who investigated a crime, and who were therefore committed to a particular view of it, should also be the prosecuting authority. What was needed was an independent body to look at the evidence with a new eye and decide what charges were justified.

The Commission's view persuaded the government, and the result was the formation of a new Crown Prosecution Service with the task of studying evidence gathered by the police and taking the decisions on whether or not to prosecute, and on what charges. Different parts of England and Wales have different starting dates for introducing the new arrangements, but the whole country will be using it by the end of 1986.

The new service will be staffed, when at full strength, by some 1,500 lawyers (both solicitors and barristers), spread around twenty-nine prosecution areas each with its own Chief Crown Prosecutor. The national head of the service is the Director of Public Prosecutions who, in turn, is responsible to the Attorney-General.

While the new system means that a fresh, independent legal mind will be looking at each case on its merits, the actual criteria for taking the decision to prosecute will not change greatly.

The prosecuting authority has a great deal of discretion. There is no obligation to prosecute whenever a crime has been committed. Indeed, prosecuting all offenders would require many times the facilities and manpower available. There may be many reasons for not prosecuting: the defendant is very old or seriously ill; he is only a trivial cog in a larger wheel and the ringleaders are not being prosecuted; the offence was committed a very long time ago. More importantly, crown prosecutors or the DPP might think that, although they are pretty sure who the criminal is, there is not quite enough evidence to get a conviction. The DPP has explained that he works to a 50 per cent rule: there must be a better chance of conviction than of acquittal.

The Crown Prosecution Service will not deal with all decisions to prosecute. For certain categories of serious crime, it is necessary to get the consent of the Attorney-General, and that has not changed under the new system. Examples include offences of terrorism and offences under the Official Secrets Act. The Attorney-General is also consulted on cases of national sensitivity or notoriety; and he retains the power to stop prosecutions already begun.

The Attorney-General and his deputy, the Solicitor-General, are politicians, appointed from among the senior barrister MPs of the party in power. Apart from his role in the courts, the Attorney-General has a political role, advising the government on legal matters and answering questions in the House of Commons. Sir Michael Havers QC is currently Attorney-General and Sir Patrick Mayhew QC, Solicitor-General.

There are all sorts of other authorities which can launch prosecutions – among them the Inland Revenue, Customs and Excise, the British Transport Police, the Department of Health and Social Security (for social security frauds) and local authorities. Private individuals as well can bring prosecutions. Private prosecutions by individuals are mainly for common assault, when the police have decided not to prosecute, but there have also been the more spectacular cases brought by Mary Whitehouse, against *Gay News* for blasphemy, and against the director of the controversial play *The Romans in Britain,* for obscenity, and the private prosecution brought by a mother against a man who supplied her son with the drugs that led to his death.

Once the decision to prosecute has been taken, the suspect can be told of it in two ways: by a charge or a summons. For serious crimes there will usually be a charge following arrest. The police will tell the suspect that he is being charged with the particular offence. Once again they must caution him that he needn't say anything. The summons is a formal document used in less serious cases, ordering the defendant to appear in court on a specified day to answer the charge against him. The summons can be served on the defendant personally, but sometimes it can even be sent by post, for minor motoring offences for instance.

## Bail

For serious crimes, the police usually arrest the suspect and keep him in detention until charging him. After being charged an accused, if not given bail by the police, must appear before a magistrates' court 'as soon as practicable', which in practice usually means the day after the charge (or two days if that day is a Sunday). The magistrates then have to decide whether to allow the accused out on bail or remand him in custody in one of the remand prisons for those awaiting trial. The law, the Bail Act 1976, says that magistrates should grant bail except in certain circumstances, the main examples being if they think that the accused is unlikely to turn up for his trial, or will interfere with witnesses, or will commit offences if let out, or needs to be in custody for his own protection.

Obviously the more serious the offence the more likely he is to disappear or nobble witnesses. Bail is rarely granted on charges of murder or armed robbery, for instance. Apart from the seriousness of the offence, the magistrates have to make the best assessment they can about the accused – his record, his job, his personal circumstances and so on. A police objection to bail will usually weigh strongly with the magistrates, but they must not refuse bail merely because the police say so; there must be a valid reason for it.

Magistrates have been criticized from both sides for their bail decisions. The police claim that they let out too many on bail, and every now and again there are claims by senior police officers and stories in the newspapers about people who commit a string of offences while out on bail. They paint a picture of gullible magistrates conned into releasing burglars and violent criminals to commit more crimes.

On the other side it is claimed that too few people are getting bail, and the picture drawn there is of thousands of innocent people languishing for weeks and months behind bars. Statistics show that more than 40 per cent of those acquitted or receiving non-custodial sentences have spent time in prison awaiting trial.

Until 1983 a defendant remanded in custody had to appear in court at least every eight days. The law has now been changed. Provided he agrees and he is legally represented, a defendant need not appear personally for twenty-eight days. The change, which was made to save money and time on ferrying remanded prisoners to and from prison, was attacked as an infringement of a basic safeguard for people in detention. The Home Secretary's answer was that it was always open to a person on remand to insist on appearing in court personally.

If magistrates grant bail they can impose conditions; for instance, that the accused must not frequent a particular pub, or must hand in his passport, or must report regularly to the police. They can ask for sureties – people who stake their own money on the expectation that the accused will turn up for his trial. If he doesn't, they can lose their money. Many trusting friends and relatives have lost their life savings this way.

## Committal

Whether a crime is tried in the magistrates' court or the Crown Court depends on its classification. Certain types of offence are 'triable either way', either summary trial by the justices, or trial by jury. Reckless driving is one such offence. Theft is another. Usually it is the defendant who has the option of deciding, though the prosecution can also express an opinion. For other specified offences, there is no choice. They are either 'summary', the less serious, tried by magistrates, or 'indictable', serious offences tried in the Crown Court. The vast majority of cases stay in the magistrates' court. But where a case is triable by the Crown Court, it cannot go there directly. It must be committed there by the magistrates' court, which has the duty to assess whether there is enough evidence to warrant sending the accused for trial by jury. In theory, only when the magistrates are satisfied that there is enough evidence – a *prima facie* case – will they commit·to the Crown Court, though in practice committal proceedings have become largely automatic.

They are supposed to be a filter through which every serious charge must pass to ensure that only genuine cases get to the higher court and that prosecutions not backed by enough evidence are stopped. The intention is that committal proceedings should be a safeguard for the defendant, to allow worthless or malicious prosecutions against him to be nipped in the bud.

They can give defendants the chance to test the prosecution evidence without giving away too much of their own case. The prosecution call their witnesses, who can then be cross-examined. Usually at the end of the prosecution evidence the defence lawyer submits that there is not enough evidence to found the charge. If the magistrates agree, the case comes to an end there and then. If the magistrates think there is enough evidence, the defence will rest its case, not call any witnesses, but have the advantage at the full trial of knowing a great deal about the prosecution case.

The disadvantage, until twenty years ago, was that such committal proceedings often used to get considerable publicity in the press and could therefore prejudice potential jurors at the trial.

In 1957 Dr John Bodkin Adams was charged with murdering an 81-year-old patient. The case excited huge public interest and the committal proceedings were given pages of publicity daily. The magistrates decided to commit for trial to the Old Bailey. When the trial started, Dr Bodkin Adams' lawyers protested that there could hardly be anyone in the country who had not read about the case and formed a view on it. Nevertheless a jury was chosen, and the members told to make up their minds on the evidence in court and to disregard anything they had read or heard previously. The jury found Dr Bodkin Adams not guilty.

But the Bodkin Adams case did eventually lead to a change in the law, in 1967. Since then, with the agreement of the defendant and his lawyer, magistrates have been able to commit him to the Crown Court without even considering the evidence. The vast majority of committals are now done in this way. Fewer than 1 per cent of defendants now go through the full 'old style' committal, and when they do the media are no longer allowed to report the proceedings unless the defendant specifically asks for publicity.

More recently, the Jeremy Thorpe case once again raised the whole issue of committal proceedings. The main controversy was over the publicity given to the committal at Minehead Magistrates' Court in Somerset. Because one of the four accused wanted the normal ban on reporting to be lifted, the magistrates had no option but to agree, even though the other three, including Mr Thorpe, would have preferred them to remain unreported. The rule has now been changed. Now, when there is disagreement between defendants about whether to allow reporting or not, the magistrates will decide.

John Smith's case is rather less spectacular. He turns up in his court with his solicitor for his straightforward automatic committal. The charge – reckless driving – is read to him. The magistrates' clerk explains that he has the choice of having the case heard before the magistrates or going to the Crown Court and having a jury trial. He goes on to tell Smith that even if he chooses summary trial before the magistrates, he may be sent to the Crown Court for sentence if the magistrates think the circumstances warrant a longer sentence than they have the power to pass. Smith answers that he wishes to be tried by a jury. His solicitor stands up to go through the formalities required – for instance, the magistrates have to make orders to make sure the witnesses turn up at the trial. The magistrates then formally commit Smith to the Crown Court. The proceedings have taken exactly five minutes.

What purpose do committal proceedings serve now? Where the defendant agrees to be committed the magistrates seem unnecessary. They no longer test the evidence. They do not even read it. They do, however, retain their sifting function when a defendant is not represented by a lawyer or where a full scale committal takes place. But even then their role appears to be minimal. Very seldom do they exercise their right of stopping the case because of insufficient evidence. Critics of the present system point to the high proportion of cases sent to the Crown Court in which the trial judge orders an acquittal because of the weakness of the evidence. That hardly suggests that the screening procedure is effective.

The Royal Commission on Criminal Procedure recommended that formal committal proceedings should be replaced by a system which would allow the defence to study the prosecution evidence long before trial, and to apply to the magistrates to discharge the accused if the evidence was too weak. The Commission also pointed out that if the decision to bring a prosecution was taken away from the police and given to an independent legally qualified official – a reform which has now taken place – the added intervention of magistrates to screen the evidence should no longer be needed. So far, however, the government has shown no signs of adopting the Commission's proposal.

## THE TRIAL

Eight centuries ago the main method of deciding guilt or innocence in England was trial by ordeal. An accused was given a red hot poker to hold, or his hands were scalded with boiling water. His injuries were immediately bandaged and the bandages were removed three days later. If the wound had healed, he was innocent; if not, he was guilty. In 1215, Pope Innocent III condemned trial by ordeal and it soon ceased to be the main mode of trial.

Trial by battle, which was current at the same time, was an even cruder device. An accused could call on his accuser (an individual in those days, not the state) to engage in a fight to the death. Astonishingly, trial by battle was not formally abolished until 1819, following a case where a bricklayer, Abraham Thornton, was accused of murder by William Ashford, the victim's brother. Thornton demanded the right to trial by battle and the courts found to their surprise that the statute granting it had not been repealed. The battle never took place, however, and Thornton eventually fled to America.

There were other primitive modes of determining innocence or guilt: getting twelve oath-swearers to confirm innocence was one. Such was the religious fear of swearing a false oath that a man's guilt could be assumed from his failure to get enough people to attest to his innocence. Another way was to make an accused swear that he was innocent, and then immediately eat some dry bread – if his oath was false, he would choke.

Trial by jury started taking over from these ancient forms from the reign of Henry II in the twelfth century. But the jury was a very different body then. It was made up of people who knew the accused – his friends and neighbours – not, as today, people who specifically ought not to know a defendant. Those who refused trial by jury for felonies (serious crimes) were forced to lie down and heavy weights were pressed on them until they consented to trial, or died. Some preferred to die, because then at least they died unconvicted and their goods passed on to their families instead of being confiscated.

But while over the centuries the criminal trial has become more sophisticated and its procedures more balanced to achieve justice, the inherent concept of a combat, a contest, has remained the feature throughout. There is a challenger – the accuser – and a defender. Instead of swords and lances the weapons are facts and legal arguments. Each side has its champion, the lawyer. There is an arbiter to make sure that the contest is fought fairly according to law.

To the casual observer the trial still appears like a strange ritual in which the judge, the lawyers and, to some extent, the court officials, are participants but the rest, including the accused and the jury, are excluded.

There are remnants of medieval language used. Judges and barristers continue to wear costumes appropriate to a different century. Above all, it becomes clear that there are two languages being spoken. The judge and barristers use one, and everyone else another. The language of the law is ultra-polite. A reprimand or criticism is delivered in such superficially amiable terms that only those who speak the language realise the sting. Senior judges are addressed as 'My Lord' (or M'Lud, as it sounds) even though they are not peers. Junior judges are 'your honour'. Barristers refer to each other as 'my learned friend', even in the heat of a dispute; a judge's opinion or remark, however ludicrous or outrageous, is always treated 'with respect' or even 'with the greatest respect', however far that may be from the truth. Lawyers speak, even when they are addressing witnesses, in an old-fashioned convoluted way seldom used in real life. The fact is that the barristers and the judge belong to the same club; they follow its rules and keep its traditions, and non-members cannot be party to the ritual. Defendants in criminal trials and litigants in civil cases are often disconcerted and upset by the apparent chumminess between lawyers who they think ought to be passionately antagonistic.

The criminal process in our 'adversarial' system concentrates heavily on what happens during the trial itself. Of course investigations have been made beforehand, mainly by the police, but also by those representing the defence. But, in contrast to the continental inquisitorial system, very little is cut and dried by the time of the trial. The verdict will depend on a combination of factors: the strength of the evidence obviously, but also the skill and persuasive abilities of the respective barristers; how the witnesses perform in the witness box (it is an unfortunate and unfair fact that a persuasive witness may not necessarily be telling the truth, and a nervous-looking, shifty, hesitant witness may be utterly honest); what impression the accused makes; how the judge controls the trial, how much he intervenes and what he includes in his summing-up; and the composition, intelligence and attitudes of the jury.

## The day of the trial

It is 10.30 in the morning, the time when Crown Courts all around the country start their main business of the day. John Smith's case is first in the list. The clerk of the court, an usher or two and the court stenographer are in their places. The barristers for the prosecution and the defence, wigged and gowned, are sitting in a row set aside for counsel. Behind the barristers sit the solicitors, or more likely their articled clerks – Mr Short, John Smith's solicitor, is too busy to come to court for such a relatively uncomplicated case. The jury box is empty. So is the dock, except for a court officer.

The judge is announced with the admonition of 'silence'. Everyone stands up. He enters from a separate door at the back of the court and sits down. The clerk of the court calls Smith's name and he comes into the dock. After confirming his identity the clerk reads the charge:

> John Smith, you are charged that on the 14th day of
> November last you drove a motor vehicle on a road,

namely Laurel Avenue, London W3, recklessly,
contrary to Section 2 of the Road Traffic Act 1972.

He ends with the time-honoured formula: 'Are you guilty or not
guilty?' John Smith answers firmly: 'Not guilty'. If he had pleaded
guilty (as more than 60 per cent of Crown Court defendants do) all
that would be left of the trial would be the procedure leading to
sentence. Smith's not guilty plea is followed by the swearing in of the
jury. When the twelve men and women have finally been sworn the
trial recommences. The clerk tells the jury what the charge against
Smith is. The preliminary stage – the overture – is ended. Act One of
the drama commences.

## The prosecution case

Mr White, the barrister for the prosecution, stands up and makes
what is called an opening speech. 'The right to begin is a priceless and
too often squandered asset,' says Richard Du Cann QC in *The Art of
the Advocate* (Pelican, 1980). Mr White explains the circumstances of
the accident, with the help of a plan, copies of which are given to the
jury. He goes on to summarize the evidence that he will call on behalf
of the prosecution. He tells them what witnesses he will call and the
gist of what they will say – or rather, what he expects them to say.
But he doesn't know for sure. A witness may not say exactly what
counsel expects, or may recant some of his evidence under cross-
examination by the defence. The whole concept of an opening
speech by the prosecution has been criticized as giving them an
unfair advantage – the jury may take more notice of what the
prosecution foretell about the evidence than what the witnesses
actually say.

After that, prosecuting counsel tells the jury that it is for the
prosecution to prove that the accused committed the crime. It is not
for the accused to prove his innocence. This is fundamental to the
English trial and the jury will be reminded of this principle many
times during the trial. Prosecution counsel explains that they must be
sure of the accused's guilt, 'beyond reasonable doubt'. After
explaining that 'burden of proof', as it is called, he gives them the
definition of reckless driving and explains what has to be proved.

MR WHITE: Well, ladies and gentlemen, there are principally two
things which you have to decide before you could come to the
conclusion that Mr Smith had driven recklessly.
   The first is that the vehicle was in fact being driven in such a
manner as to create an obvious and serious risk of causing
physical harm. If your answer to that question is yes, you are
quite sure, when you've heard all the facts, that the driving
was indeed obviously creating a serious risk, then you go on to

consider the second question, which is equally important, but different.

And that second question is this: was the defendant in fact driving without having given any thought to the possibility of there being such a risk, or, having recognized that there was some risk, had he nonetheless gone on to take it? So there you have to look at, as best you can, the defendant's mind.

The prosecution's opening speech may take less than an hour or it may, in a complicated case, take up several hours or even days. When counsel has finished he starts calling his witnesses.

They will usually include a police officer or two, the victim of the crime, and any witnesses who can shed light on it, eye-witnesses particularly. There may also be expert witnesses, on fingerprints for instance. In John Smith's case there are only three witnesses – the policeman at the scene; Anne Jones, the injured victim; and Mrs Wright, who was about to cross Laurel Avenue when John Smith passed in his car. She claims he was going at excessive speed and nearly knocked her over.

The witnesses first take the oath, according to the customs of their religion, or they solemnly affirm, if they are non-believers. The Christian oath, the one most widely taken, states: 'I swear by almighty God that the evidence I shall give shall be the truth, the whole truth and nothing but the truth.' (There is no 'So help me God'.)

The questions put to a witness and the answers he gives are collectively known as examination-in-chief. This is where the prosecution elicits the basic facts. It is a cardinal rule that the barrister must not put words into his witness' mouth; he must not, as it is called, 'lead' his witness. It is in order for Mr Brown to ask Mrs Wright what happened next and get the reply: 'The accused's car nearly knocked me over.' But he is not entitled to ask: 'Did the accused's car nearly knock you over?' That would be a leading question, and not allowed.

Prosecution counsel's task is to elicit all the relevant facts from the witnesses – his duty is not to extract simply the evidence damaging to the accused. The law steps in to stop the witness from saying something which he does not know for himself – 'hearsay' evidence. This is what the witness has heard from someone else, not something which he can vouch for himself. For instance, a witness' evidence that someone told him that Smith was driving fast because he was in a hurry would not be admissible.

In John Smith's case neither the policeman's evidence nor that of Anne Jones will be controversial. Mrs Jones remembers very little of the accident. Mrs Wright's evidence, however, is potentially damaging, because it suggests that Smith was driving far too fast even before the events leading to the accident.

MRS WRIGHT: Well I decided that I'd cross the road, just a few yards
    down from my home, and go across to the other side of the
    road, and this van passed me. And I was just about to cross
    when this red car came zooming past – nearly knocked me
    down actually . . .

The object of cross-examination is simple: it is to destroy,
discredit or at least cast doubt on the evidence of the other side's
witness, and in weakening his case to enhance your own side's. The
art of cross-examination is not easy. In the hands of a skilled
practitioner it is a sleek rapier delicately thrusting, testing, tempting,
looking for an opening and, when finding one, directing the blade
home cleanly and irrevocably. But in the hands of an inexperienced
or second-rate advocate, it is more like a blunderbuss, peppering shot
everywhere, almost at random, occasionally, through luck and
statistical probability, hitting a target, but often causing much
damage on the way. Cross-examination is bounded by a host of
detailed rules about what the cross-examiner may and may not ask.
He is, however, free to ask leading questions, an important tool in his
attempt to break down the witness. The cross-examination is rarely
as quickly effective and as crude as it is portrayed in television
drama. Witnesses seldom fall to pieces because of one question.
Rather it is the accumulation of threads which, when skilfully woven
together, portray to the jury a witness whose evidence, seeming so
strong a little while ago. suddenly appears unreliable, possibly
mistaken or even, perhaps, untruthful.

Defence counsel, Mr Brown, is anxious to demonstrate to the jury
that Mrs Wright is not a witness they should believe. He asks her to
estimate the speeds and distances; he puts to her contradictions
between her statement to the police and her evidence in court.

When defence counsel has finished cross-examining the witness,
prosecution counsel is entitled to re-examine, to try to clear up, and
put in the best light, any new matter that has come out of cross-
examination, and to recover any ground that might have been lost.

And so the prosecution case continues: examination in chief of
prosecution witnesses, cross-examination by the defence and
possible re-examination by the prosecution.

The judge can and often does intervene to ask questions of his own
when he is not clear on a point, or to supplement a line of questioning
started by the barristers. But a judge must not take over the case. Our
adversarial system requires that the combatants should be the
prosecution and the defence – the judge should not himself descend
into the arena.

The first scene of Act One draws to a close. Prosecution counsel
has finished calling his witnesses and formally announces: 'That is the
case for the prosecution.'

# The defence case

It is now the defence's turn. But before calling his witnesses the defence counsel has a chance of ending the whole trial there and then by persuading the judge (in the absence of the jury) that the prosecution has not even produced enough evidence to warrant going further. There is no case to meet, he suggests; no reasonable jury could convict on the evidence that the prosecution has put forward. There is no *prima facie* case. Defence counsel will obviously minimise the effect of the evidence which has been given, while the prosecution barrister will emphasise its strength. If the judge decides in favour of the defence, he will call the jury in and tell them formally to acquit the accused. Otherwise, the case goes on. (Even then defence counsel may choose to call no witnesses in the confidence that the prosecution has not discharged the burden of proof, and therefore that the jury will be bound to find in favour of the accused.)

In John Smith's case there is no point in suggesting that there is no case to answer – the fact that he has knocked down a pedestrian while travelling on the wrong side of the road is at least a *prima facie* indication of careless or reckless driving.

Mr Brown opens the defence case by calling John Smith as his first witness. He does not make an opening speech. Unless the accused is going to be the only witness, defence counsel are entitled to outline their case, just as the prosecution do for the other side. But they often forgo their right. Except in a complicated case, a defence opening address is usually considered unnecessary.

The accused is usually the first witness called. But there is no obligation on him to give evidence at all. He has the right to say nothing. He may decide not to give evidence for tactical reasons, because he thinks the prosecution has not proved the case against him; or it may be that his lawyer thinks he will put up an unconvincing show in the witness-box. The jury, however, may take the view – though they are not supposed to – that any accused who does not give evidence has something to hide.

The accused is followed by the witnesses in support of his case. The procedure of the first part of the trial is reversed: defence counsel examines his witnesses and then prosecution counsel has the chance to cross-examine them, to try to undo or reverse any harm to his case that defence counsel may have done. There may be re-examination by the defence, and some questions from the judge.

John Smith's own evidence is aimed at trying to persuade the jury that he was not driving recklessly. He claims that he was placed in an unforeseeable emergency and had to take evading action, because of the van that suddenly swerved left and the motor cycle that appeared from Cornwallis Road.

JOHN SMITH: I was thinking about overtaking, and at that point the
van moved out suddenly to the right, and then swung away
quickly to the left, without any signal. And this manoeuvre by
the van prompted me to swing quickly to the right and avoid
it.

As I overtook the van, as I drew level with it, a motor
cyclist suddenly appeared right in front of me. I'm assuming it
came from my left, although I never saw it actually move. It
was suddenly in front of me – I was slightly towards the crown
of the road, and the motor cycle was dead in front of me, at
this point, just a matter of yards, and I jammed my foot on the
brakes and turned quickly to the right, and began to skid. I
missed the motor cycle . . .

Later, Mr Brown asks him: 'What caused you to brake and swerve in
the manner we've heard about?

JOHN SMITH: The combination of the sudden manoeuvre of the van,
and the appearance of the motor cyclist directly in front of me.

He is cross-examined by Mr White, who suggests that he was
driving at excessive speed, that he should not have overtaken the van
in the first place, and that, had he been driving at normal speed, he
would have avoided the accident.

MR WHITE: You see what I'm putting to you, Mr Smith, is that in fact
your speed was such that the van slowing down and turning to
the left either meant you ran into the back of the van, because
you were too close, going too fast; or you had to do what you
did, which was to swing out on to the wrong side of the road,
without really being able to see what was coming. Now isn't
that really what happened?

He then concentrates his cross-examination on the motor cycle:

Mr Smith, you've heard the two witnesses giving their evidence, Mrs Wright particularly, saying she didn't see any
motor cycle. Are you sure there was a motor cycle there?

JOHN SMITH: There would have been no other reason for me to
brake. Or to swerve.

MR WHITE (a little later): You see I suggest to you, Mr Smith, that
this motor cycle is really a figment of your imagination,
something you've conjured up to explain why you took the
action you did. Isn't that right?

Smith denies this firmly.

Now to the surprise of the prosecution, the next witness is Timothy Wood, the driver of the blue van, who has only just been traced, partly the result of hard work by Smith's solicitor, Mr Short, and an inquiry agent, and partly through luck. Wood confirms Smith's story about the motor bike – up to that time one of the crucial elements of the case. There is little Mr White can do in cross-examination. One of the mainstays of his case has been undermined. The van driver is the second and last witness for the defence. The defence case is formally closed.

## Closing speeches

The witnesses have gone, the witness box is empty. The jury have been told all the evidence they need (or rather, all they are going to hear, which under the adversarial system may well amount to less than all the relevant evidence). It is now time for the barristers to take centre stage with no-one to interrupt them. Prosecuting counsel is first. The defence then has the last word. It is the defence case that will be the more recent in the jury's mind, unless it is undone by the judge's summing-up which follows.

Both barristers will have the same objective: to summarize their side's case in its most favourable light; to highlight its strengths, play down its weaknesses; to boost the evidence given by their own witnesses and pick holes in the opposition's evidence. In the not too distant past, even up to thirty years ago, a closing speech was the occasion for advocates to rise to the heights of their oratorical powers. This was the part of the trial when the spotlight was on them and them alone, the chance to use all their verbal skills, their thespian talents, their powers to evoke sympathy and emotion, all to the service of their client. Usually it was the defence lawyer who had the best lines, but he also had the greatest responsibility. A poor performance on his part might mean the gallows for his client. In that atmosphere thrived some of England's greatest advocates – Carson, Marshall Hall, Birkett, Hastings. It was Hall who finished his speech in defence of a pathetic ageing prostitute accused of murder, with the exhortation:

> Look at her, gentlemen of the jury. Look at her. God
> never gave her a chance – won't you?

Can there have been a dry eye in the jury box? Whatever the effect such perorations had on the juries of yesteryear, they would probably only bring ridicule today. The new generation of barristers are perhaps more careful with their facts, more clinical in their analysis, more meticulous in their preparation, but utterly grey in their presentation to the jury. Richard Du Cann QC, one of England's most elegant advocates, bemoans the increasing number of counsel who 'stumble through the odious task of addressing the judge, boring themselves almost as much as their audience.'

The points to be made in John Smith's case are obvious.

FOR THE PROSECUTION: But ladies and gentlemen, isn't this really the situation – given the speed that you know he was travelling at, is it not simply that he had failed to give himself sufficient distance behind the van, and that when the emergency arose, and it wasn't you may think a particularly uncommon or extraordinary circumstance, he was simply going too fast to do the obvious and safe thing, which was to slow down in his own lane by braking, until the road was clear. Ladies and gentlemen, you may think if he'd done that, he would never have needed to leave his side of the road, and no accident would in fact have taken place . . .

His evidence, and it's quite unequivocal in my submission, is that he was forced to take evasive action by the action of the van and the motor cycle. Prosecution would suggest to you that really the only reason he had to take evasive action was because he was going too fast to do the sensible and reasonable thing, of slowing down.

FOR THE DEFENCE: This defendant is faced with a very real emergency. He puts on his brakes; he avoids the motor cyclist, the motor cyclist carries on, and this defendant – doing the best he can, we submit – brakes but unfortunately strikes the unfortunate lady who you saw give evidence.

Members of the jury, can you really say that in the circumstances this defendant was driving in such a way as to create an obvious and serious risk of injury? He was faced, in our submission, with these two unforeseen circumstances. First of all, he didn't know the van was going to turn, there was no indication.

Second unforeseen circumstance: the motor cycle, waiting at the junction of Cornwallis Road, pulls out quite suddenly and quite wrongly into the main road, immediately in front of the defendant.

Members of the jury, bearing in mind all the circumstances of this case, we submit to you that the case is very far from being made out against this defendant . . .

In all the circumstances, I submit to you that there's only one proper verdict in this case, and this is one of Not Guilty. Thank you.

Prosecution and defence counsel have finished their speeches, but the jury is not yet free. It is now time for the judge to address them.

## The judge's summing-up

The jury has heard an opening and a closing speech for the prosecution, a closing speech by the defence and a procession of witnesses giving evidence and being cross-examined. It might be thought that the issues in the case were firmly fixed in their minds. But they are to hear more. The judge is to sum up the case to them. What function does the summing-up serve?

First, its importance lies in the fact that it comes from an impartial independent source. The prosecution and the defence are the combatants, each fighting for their cause. They are not and cannot be expected to be impartial in their presentation of the case. The judge, on the other hand, is an independent figure, who can be trusted to summarize the main issues of the case impartially.

Second, the jury is made up of laymen, not lawyers. But some of the decisions they may have to make involve some appreciation of the legal niceties: what is the dividing line between reckless driving and careless driving? How vital is it that the person *intends* to commit the crime with which he is charged? Again, a judge is a better guide through this legal minefield than counsel. Third, it is especially helpful in a long trial to have someone of experience highlighting the main points of the evidence which the jury may have forgotten because they were raised several days before and have not been mentioned by either counsel in closing speeches.

The judge will usually start by reminding the jury of the two essential aspects of the English criminal trial. First, that it is for the jury and only the jury to decide questions of fact and to make up their minds between the versions that have been put forward by the competing interests. The judge's role is limited to deciding legal issues and he should not trespass into the jury's province and express obvious views on the facts or the witnesses, and certainly not on the result. He sometimes does so, but the jury is entitled to, and should, disregard his opinion.

Second, the judge repeats that it is for the prosecution to prove guilt, so that the jury are sure of it, and not for the defence to prove innocence:

JUDGE: You could come to the conclusion – and I'm not going to say to you that you should, because that's a matter entirely for you – you might come to the conclusion that he was innocent of any offence at all, in which case the verdict would be Not Guilty.

Secondly, you might come to the conclusion that although there was a strong suspicion, there was a reasonable doubt, and if there's a reasonable doubt in a case, well then the defendant is entitled to be acquitted.

The third possibility is that you might be satisfied so that you're sure that an offence had been committed, and if it has been committed, then it's your duty in accordance with your oaths to find a verdict of Guilty.

The judge then defines the law of the offence charged. It may be simple. The definition of, say, burglary, is relatively easy to explain. But where there are several charges, some of them alternatives to each other – murder and manslaughter for instance – it becomes very important for the judge to make his explanations clear. If he gets it wrong and misleads the jury on the law, it could be the basis for a successful appeal.

In John Smith's case there is an important legal point to be made. Although Smith has been charged with reckless driving, the jury is entitled to acquit him on that, and yet find him guilty of the lesser charge of careless driving. What is the difference? The judge explains:

JUDGE: If you come to the conclusion that this defendant deliberately shut his mind to the consequences, or knowing that there was a danger, went on to undertake it – that's reckless. Careless driving is an absolute offence, whatever the person concerned is thinking, provided it's a deliberate act and even though the defendant was doing his incompetent best, it was a careless thing to do: careless in respect of speed, careless in respect of the way he was trying to pass that vehicle in the circumstances. If his method of driving was such that it was a conscious act and it was careless, although his mind didn't go with it as regards the consequences, that still would be careless driving.

After explaining the law, the judge summarizes what he sees as the main points of the evidence. Throughout the trial he has taken notes (usually in laborious longhand, one of the reasons why trials take so long) and goes through these notes reminding the jury of the main factual issues. If there is more than one defendant, he must be particularly careful that he correctly distinguishes what evidence applies to which defendant.

At the end of his summing-up – which may take anything from a few minutes to a few days – he tells the jury that they must try to reach a unanimous verdict. It will only be hours later, if the jury have not been able to agree on their decision, that the judge may call them back to tell them that they can reach a majority verdict by a margin of ten to two or eleven to one.

The judge leaves the court. The jury file out. The accused is led away from the dock. The lawyers chat a little among themselves and slowly make their way out, as do the accused's friends and relatives and other spectators. The court is virtually empty. Outside it, the main participants and interested parties mill around. There is time for a cup of tea, but they cannot stay away too long in case of a speedy verdict. The curtain comes down on the first act.

## The verdict

The second act takes place almost entirely behind closed doors. The twelve members of the jury are taken to the room in which, in secret, they will reach their verdict. There they will stay for minutes, hours, or even days (in which case they will be taken to a hotel to spend the night). In John Smith's trial, the jury need only an hour for their deliberations. They reach a unanimous verdict and tell the jury bailiff that they are ready to come back to court. The word spreads. The judge and the barristers are found. John Smith is brought back into the dock. The judge sits down and the jury file in.

COURT USHER: Will the foreman please stand. Will you please confine yourself to answering my first question, yes or no. Has the jury reached a verdict upon which you are all agreed?
FOREMAN: We have.
USHER: Do you find the defendant John Smith guilty or not guilty of reckless driving?
FOREMAN: Not guilty.
USHER: Do you find the defendant guilty or not guilty of careless driving?
FOREMAN: Guilty.
USHER: Is that the verdict of you all?
FOREMAN: It is.
USHER: Yes, do sit down.

## JURIES

An essential bulwark against oppression or an inefficient anachronism? Lord Devlin put it at its highest in *Trial By Jury* (Methuen, 1966):

> The first object of any tyrant in Whitehall would be to make Parliament utterly subservient to his will; and the next to overthrow or diminish trial by jury, for no tyrant could afford to leave a subject's freedom in the hands of twelve of his countrymen. So that trial by jury is more than an instrument of justice and more than one

wheel of the constitution: it is the lamp that shows that freedom lives.

Sir Sebag Shaw, one of the top criminal barristers before he became a judge:

> A jury as at present constituted and composed and brought together, in a sense by the chance of being on the same jury panel at the same time, is the right kind of body to try criminal cases.
>
> It has the great merit and advantage of being anonymous and amorphous. Once the trial is over it's dissolved and there is no person responsible to anybody or answerable for the decision. It can therefore be much more independent. It hasn't got to consider what people will think about it as an individual, as a judge might think about how the public will regard him as an individual, if he were to come to a wrong verdict.

But Professor Brian Hogan of Leeds University, one of the leading academic experts on criminal law, puts the opposite view:

> In my view, trial by jury has long outlived its usefulness. We preserve it because it's a sacred cow. It's been with us for so long and we're failing to look carefully into it, to see what it does, and to see whether there are rational grounds for defending it.
>
> If we'd never had trial by jury in this country and our practice had been to try cases by judges, rationally finding the facts and drawing inferences, and I were to come boldly along with the suggestion that this professional judgment should be replaced by an almost inscrutable verdict, by the first twelve men and women you meet in the street, I think any sensible person would believe that I'd gone out of my mind.

Professor Glanville Williams of Cambridge University, another distinguished legal academic, takes much the same view. The police too, who admittedly have a particular interest to defend, have over the past decade largely turned against the jury system.

It is not just a question of lawyers and judges versus academics and the police. Supporters and detractors of the system are to be found in all camps, including jurors themselves. Nor is it a stark question of the jury's survival or its abolition. Some of the criticisms could easily be met by reforms of particular aspects of the system, without the need to kill the institution altogether.

Juries have been around for 800 years, but their functions and composition have changed considerably over that period. Juries in civil trials have all but disappeared, except for the occasional libel case or false imprisonment. In 1981 a civil jury sat for nearly six months on a libel suit in which the Moonies failed to persuade them that the sect had been defamed by the *Daily Mail*. In 1986 a civil jury turned down miners' leader Arthur Scargill's claim for false imprisonment against the police. He had alleged that police action against him following an alleged speeding offence was unlawful. The jury decided otherwise after a ten-day trial and Mr Scargill was saddled with heavy costs.

More important is the change in the membership of the jury in criminal trials that has come about over the years, and especially since 1973. The theory is that juries are supposed to be chosen at random as representatives of the community, but this has never been so in practice. Before 1973 there was an age qualification and a property qualification. A juror had to be between twenty-one and sixty and a house owner or ratepayer. This test discriminated against women, mainly because most married couples had their houses in the husband's name rather than the wife's, and against the young, who were not householders. A pre-1973 jury was therefore predominantly male and middle-aged – hardly representative of the community.

This has changed dramatically. Now jury service is based on the electoral roll, which means that an eighteen-year-old can serve on a jury, though there is an upper limit of sixty-five. Outside London, selection is now done by computer, according to a formula confirmed by the Royal Statistical Society as delivering a random result.

There are categories of people who cannot serve on a jury: judges, magistrates, lawyers, the police, prison warders and other connected with the administration of justice; the clergy; the mentally ill. Other categories are eligible but in practice are automatically exempted: members of the Armed Forces, MPs, peers of the realm, doctors, nurses and others in the medical field. And anyone can be excused because of particular personal circumstances: the blind or deaf, for instance; mothers with very small children; people running one-man businesses and so on. A lot depends on the clerk at the particular court. Some will allow people off jury service if it interferes with an arranged holiday: others are more strict.

Finally, no one with a serious criminal record is supposed to sit on a jury. Anyone who has had imposed on him a sentence of imprisonment (even if the sentence has been suspended), or youth custody, or community service within the previous ten years is disqualified, as are those who, within the past five years have been given probation. But this means that it is possible for criminals with lengthy records who have not actually been to prison for three months to become jurors. The government has announced its intention to change the law to disqualify anyone convicted of certain crimes for which they could have gone to prison, even if they did not actually spend any time in custody.

A typical jury today is likely to be much younger, have a closer ratio of men to women and have more working-class members than one of ten years ago. This is not to everyone's liking. The first objection is to the eighteen-year-old limit. Barry Pain, a former Chief Constable of Kent, put it this way:

> I believe quite sincerely that eighteen is far too young an age to select a juror. Yes, I know they can go in the army and fight for their country at eighteen. Yes, I know they've got the vote at eighteen. But quite honestly I do believe that at eighteen a youngster has been protected by his parents or by his school or by his university; he hasn't yet had the chance to go out and earn his living and face all the trauma that entails, and I believe he's immature to the degree that he is not capable of giving a mature judgement on a set of facts pro and con, placed before him in a courtroom.

Some judges and barristers take the view that the lower age limit should be twenty-five. Lord Denning's criticism takes a different line, in *What Next in the Law* (Butterworths, 1982):

> Nowadays virtually every member of the population is qualified to sit as a juror. No matter how illiterate or uneducated or unsuitable he may be. And where the chances, by sheer weight of numbers, are loaded heavily against the jurors being the sensible and responsible members of the community ... There should be a qualification for service as a juror so that a jury is composed of sensible and responsible members of the community. It should be representative of the best of them of whatever sex or colour, and of whatever age or occupation. Service as a juror should be regarded as a service to the community – as indeed it is. It should command the respect of the people generally – much as service as a magistrate does now. Those on the jury list should be selected in much the same way as magistrates are now. Sometimes people apply. Sometimes they are recommended by others. Always references are required. Interviews are held to assess suitability.

The other point made about the new juries is that their level of comprehension of cases, and perhaps their level of intelligence, are lower than they used to be. Under the previous system, it is argued, it could be assumed that jurors, most of whom owned houses, were probably earning and had demonstrated some degree of responsibility and understanding. Serving on a jury today, which still requires no educational qualification, is more open to the irresponsible and to those not up to doing the job. There is not even a language or comprehension requirement to ensure that jurors who are called up at least understand the cases they have to try.

A jury panel is finally assembled at the court. How many are summoned will depend on the particular court they are being called to. The Old Bailey, with nineteen courts normally sitting at one time, has between 300 and 400 jurors on the premises on any given day, both sitting on cases and waiting around. Smaller courthouses gear their numbers to their needs. The long uncomfortable wait begins. (It is a recurring criticism of the system that it pays so little regard to jurors' comfort and does so little to tell them what is going on.) Eventually a batch of jurors is called to a particular court, but it will not necessarily be the first twelve who become the jury.

The law allows another assault on the principle of randomness which can lead to unbalanced and unrepresentative juries. A defendant is allowed three 'peremptory challenges' – he can reject three potential jurors without giving any reasons. It does not matter much when there is only one accused, but each defendant can have his three challenges, so where there are several they can materially affect the kind of jury they get. In 1980, twelve black defendants charged with offences stemming from riots in St. Paul's, Bristol, used up thirty-five of their thirty-six challenges before reaching a jury that suited them, including five blacks and Asians. In 1982, fifteen young blacks, charged in connection with the death of a white youth, Terry May, in London, eventually ended up with a jury in which only five of the twelve were white. But to do that they had to challenge thirty-seven jurors originally, and another twenty-six after the trial had to be restarted when it was discovered that a juror was related to defence counsel. Their action was perfectly legal and, moreover, there is no evidence at all that the jury so chosen did anything other than their duty. If the defendants in the Terry May case were hoping that a predominantly black and Asian jury would be more prone to let them off, they were disappointed: many of them were convicted.

But there is concern about the use of challenges to get rid of everyone who looks vaguely respectable or establishment, or wears a suit and tie, in order to get an unrepresentative jury more likely, in the mind of the accused, to let him off.

The prosecution too have the right to challenge without cause, though they exercise the right more sparingly. The procedure is different, but the result is the same. Prosecuting counsel calls on a juror to 'stand by for the Crown', which means he goes to the back of the queue of potential jurors and in effect is never called again.

Both prosecution and defence also have an unlimited right to challenge for cause – to reject a juror for a particular reason. Many critics would like to limit jury challenges to challenges for cause. Chief Constable Barry Pain:

> I do think it reasonable, on behalf of the community as a whole, which the jury is supposed to be serving, for reasons for objecting to a juror to be given to the court, to make sure they're valid reasons and not just because a man looks as if he may bring in a verdict which is contrary to what the defence counsel wants.

There is a difficulty in limiting challenges in this way. How is the defence, in particular, to know whether there is something about the juror that justifies a challenge? In the United States a juror can be questioned at length about his beliefs and prejudices. Psychiatrists can be employed to assess potential jurors, and private detectives to rummage around their neighbourhood and workplace. In the trial of black activist Bobby Seale in 1971, no fewer than 1,035 jurors were rejected before the final twelve were selected. The process took four months. All this is foreign to the English system, but there have been instances of jury 'vetting', especially by the prosecution. It was revealed in 1978 that for certain kinds of trials, involving terrorism or criminal gangs, for example, the police and Special Branch searched their files for background information about potential jury members, and made further enquiries about them. Prosecution counsel was given the information so that he could challenge the jurors. The material passed on was not just about criminal activity or association. Some of it referred to perfectly legal conduct, such as taking part in demonstrations or being friendly with squatters. The incidence of vetting of this kind appears to have decreased, though the practice of checking police records, to make sure that no disqualified criminal sits on a jury, is widespread.

The government has announced its intention of reducing the defendant's right to peremptory challenge, to two or one for each defendant, or even abolishing the right altogether. At the time of writing, it has yet to announce which of the options it intends to bring before Parliament.

The twelve who finally emerge from the selection process are now sworn. They promise: 'I will faithfully try the several issues joined between our sovereign lady the Queen and the prisoner at the Bar, and give a true verdict according to the evidence.'

The trial begins. The jury sit through, in silence, the speeches, the evidence, the cross-examination and finally, the judge's summing-up which is specifically addressed to them. They do not interrupt and seldom ask questions, although they are entitled to do so if they wish something to be clarified. They can take notes if they want to. The jury are given some of the documents in the case, but not necessarily all of them. The judge, at the end of his summing-up, emphasizes that the jury must try to reach a unanimous verdict. If they find they cannot reach a twelve-nil decision, the judge may, after giving them an opportunity to agree, call them back and tell them he will accept a majority verdict of ten-two, or eleven-one. How long a judge will wait before telling them about the majority verdict depends on the complexity of the case, but it must not be less than two hours. It could be several hours more than that.

What actually happens in a jury room is supposed to be a secret, and now the Contempt of Court Act 1981 has made it even more difficult to find out. It is now unlawful for a juror to reveal the secrets of the discussion in the jury room, or for a newspaper or anyone else to try to get the information by interviewing a juror.

But we do have some idea. Several jurors wrote about their experiences before it was forbidden, and many others have talked about it. There have also been research studies, using 'shadow' juries – made up of ordinary members of the public who have been chosen in the normal way, attended a real case and then pretended to be the real jury. Their discussions were observed and noted by researchers. (And of course there is the film *Twelve Angry Men* which, for anyone who has not been on a jury is probably the main, though highly misleading, reference point for what goes on when a jury retires).

Our information is therefore mainly anecdotal, with academic research a secondary source. Not surprisingly, the anecdotes told about jury experiences are many and varied and there is a vast division of opinion about the system. Horrific tales are related of the inability of jurors to understand the most basic points, of their total silence throughout, of a bully's hectoring the others into submission, of a pressing dinner engagement determining which way a juror voted, and of sheer prejudice – against blacks, policemen, Irish or the young. A woman juror in Croydon managed to get taken off the jury altogether when she revealed that she was extremely prejudiced. But there will be just as many stories about how conscientiously a jury debated the issue, how closely they followed the evidence, how much time they devoted to sifting each detail, how they stuck to the facts and refused to make assumptions based on prejudice.

The truth about juries is that, like judges and magistrates, there are some very good ones and some bad ones, just as one would expect from such a random exercise. There will inevitably be some people who play a bigger part in the discussion than others, some who will understand the legal nuances and the facts better, some who will tend to believe the police and others who will be much more defence-minded, some who will be more patient than others. There is very little evidence, anecdotal or otherwise, to suggest that there is anything fundamentally unsatisfactory in the way juries reach their verdicts.

Different juries approach their task in different ways, even from the very first decision – choosing one of them as foreman. There are no set rules, so the jury muddle through as best they can. Some juries pick someone among them who, by dress, accent or general appearance perhaps, seems (rightly or wrongly) competent at running things. Others prefer to go for someone who has been on a jury before, and therefore is assumed to know the ropes. Or it may be done by names in a hat, or volunteering. Nor are there any set rules for the foreman. He can conduct the discussion in whatever way he thinks best, from a formal chairman approach to a free-for-all.

The way juries approach a case is often equally unsystematic. Dr Philip Sealy of the London School of Economics has studied some hundreds of shadow juries. He found that juries do not necessarily work through the evidence systematically in the order it was given. They do not always discuss the burden of proof – the presumption of innocence – which is at the heart of the system. They do not always fully understand the legal distinctions explained to them (between reckless and careless driving in Smith's case, for instance). But in the end, they usually get the facts right and they often get the right result according to the law, even if they have imperfectly understood it.

Does it matter that they don't always understand all the legal technicalities? Lord Elwyn-Jones, former Lord Chancellor, doesn't think so:

> They get a lot of advice in the course of a trial. They've got the advice of the prosecuting counsel; they've got the eloquent advice of defending counsel; and of course the overall supervision by the judge, who gives guidance as the case proceeds, and does his best to see that the jury are following what they've got to decide in the end – the guilt or innocence of the accused – and then he finally sums up, explaining the issues, and the law. At the close of the trial, they're pretty well equipped to apply their commonsense to the question. . . And my experience of juries is that broadly speaking they get the right result.

What matters is not so much that every member of the jury should understand every nuance of the law and every factual detail, but that they should in the end use their collective commonsense to reach a correct conclusion.

The crucial question is whether or not they get it right. It is not easy to tell. People who are wrongly acquitted are hardly likely to advertise the jury's mistake. The police believe that juries often do acquit the guilty, but this is not necessarily a point against the jury: it probably has more to do with the law of evidence which, to the police's great distress, allows a suspect to keep silent during the police interrogation without having it count against him at his subsequent trial. Nor can we assess how often juries wrongly convict from the number of successful appeals against their verdicts. Because juries never give reasons for their decisions, it is often very difficult to find a ground of appeal. Unless there is new evidence, the only way to upset a jury's verdict is to find something wrong with the trial itself, for instance, an irregularity in the proceedings, or the judge's misleading summing-up or evidence allowed that should have been ruled inadmissible. It is impossible to go behind a jury's verdict and it is not enough for an appellant just to claim that the jury were wrong. It is quite possible, perhaps probable, that juries have mistakenly convicted people where no appeal was possible because no specific ground for appeal could be found.

Two lecturers at Birmingham University, Dr John Baldwin and Dr Michael McConville, have done a great deal of research into juries and are widely accepted as the leading academic authorities on the working of the system. In 1977 they conducted a survey to try to assess how many wrongful verdicts juries reached. They looked at 370 trials in Birmingham and spoke to the trial judge, prosecution and defence counsel, and often the police officer in charge of the case. They compared the views of those participants with the actual verdicts reached. For the most part they tallied, but in a surprisingly large number of cases – 56 of the 370 – the trial judge and at least one other party disagreed with the jury's conclusion. This does not of course necessarily mean that the jury was wrong and the judge always right. In most cases where other participants in the trial disagreed with the jury's verdict, the judge would have convicted where the jury decided the defendant was not guilty. But in some cases it was the other way around. The jury found the defendant guilty when the judge, and sometimes even the police officer, would have acquitted. Even making all allowances, that survey suggests that if the Birmingham figures are applied throughout the country, hundreds of people are being wrongly convicted by juries every year. That in itself does not necessarily damn the jury system. Would the number of wrongful convictions be fewer under any other system? No criminal justice process in the world can ever be foolproof.

If we believe the jury system to be inadequate, what are we to put in its place? Professor Hogan believes that juries are being asked to do something which is essentially a professional task:

> To find facts, and – this is more important – draw the
> appropriate inferences from fact. I believe those matters

to call for professional skills and professional judgement, which the jury does not have.

He favours trial by judge alone, as in civil trials:

> The judge tells us the story of the case, he finds the facts. He says which persons he believed, which persons he did not believe, and he puts the story together, and he draws the appropriate inferences. . . The convicted accused in the criminal case would know why he had been convicted, what was regarded as important and what was regarded as unimportant. He would be, so far as an appeal is concerned, in a stronger position.

Views like Professor Hogan's are gaining significant ground. But those who would wish to abolish the jury altogether are still in a small minority and there is no agreement about how to replace it. Some for instance would have a judge with two lay assessors; others a judge with magistrates; still others a judge sitting on his own. Defenders of the jury system say that the judge would become too case-hardened, that he would be unable to take a fresh look at every case before him. A jury, by contrast, have none of the preconceptions born of too many years doing the same job.

Perhaps more importantly, juries have a value above that of the verdicts they deliver. They are the direct link between the ordinary person and the administration of justice. The jury system provides a vital element of community participation in the workings of our society. It is a necessary reassurance that justice is not meted out by a remote elite but is something in which every citizen in a democratic society can play a part.

Juries are important, too, as a barometer of public feeling on the state of the law. They can and do express their displeasure about a particular law or a particular prosecution by refusing to convict, as they did when Clive Ponting was prosecuted under the Official Secrets Act for leaking information about the background to the Falklands War. It is mainly because juries were refusing to convict publishers charged with publishing obscene books that the law has all but fallen into disuse. In the past their role has been much more dramatic. In the latter days of the death penalty in Britain they were often reluctant to convict of murder, even when the facts bore out the charge, because of a likelihood that the accused, for whom they might have had some sympathy, would be hanged. Even longer ago, it was the refusal of juries to find defendants guilty of sheep stealing which caused it to be removed from the list of capital crimes. Lord Elwyn-Jones:

> The value of the jury in protecting the citizen in that way and in putting some control over the power of the

executive to impose and try to inflict unjust criminal laws on the community, the presence of those twelve men and women – the palladium of our liberty – to decide his fate ultimately is very important.

It is arguable, however, that this function is no longer as important as it used to be. Our laws are less stringent than they were, our fundamental civil liberties are not as much under attack, and when they are, there are other bodies to defend them.

One issue in particular has given rise to controversy. Many argue that a jury is not an appropriate body for determining guilt or innocence in long and complicated fraud trials, or other cases which require the detailed inspection of accounts and figures. First, such cases tend to be inordinately long – several weeks or even several months: one case lasted 137 working days, followed by a re-trial lasting the same length of time. Second, they require a high degree of numeracy and special financial understanding from a jury which is not chosen with those qualities in mind. Often the accountants and the financial experts are at odds about the figures; the judge is frequently at sixes and sevens. How can a jury of ordinary men and women possibly cope? The Fraud Trials Committee, under the chairmanship of Lord Roskill, a law lord, agreed with these points. In a report published in 1986, the Committee proposed that in especially complex fraud trials the jury should be replaced by a judge and two lay members with knowledge and experience of financial dealings. The government, at the time of writing, has not yet decided whether to implement that recommendation.

Otherwise, for the foreseeable future, the jury system is firmly entrenched. It may be the subject of further calls for reform, especially of the age qualifications, the right to peremptory challenges and perhaps the need for some sort of language or comprehension test. It may be tinkered with, but it is a reasonably safe bet that it will be there, more or less as we know it today, in the next century.

## THE SENTENCE

A trial is not always successful drama. Its structure often demands an anti-climax. The curtains falls on the second act with a dramatic exit line from the jury: their verdict of guilty or not guilty. (In practice, even this is messy – there are often many charges and several defendants to get through and the verdict-taking can last several minutes.) But the play only ends there if the accused has been acquitted. The final curtain can then descend amid scenes of joyful tears and jubilation. If the verdict is guilty, the actors have to play another act – the sentence.

The sentencing process does not only take place after a full-blown trial: the accused may have pleaded guilty at the start. If there has been a trial the judge and the public will of course know all the evidence. With a guilty plea, however, nothing is known except the bald charge and in those cases prosecution counsel will give a short outline of the main facts of the offence. No witnesses are called. From then on the procedure is the same as with conviction by a jury.

First, the prosecution provides the judge with information about the accused's previous criminal record, if he has one, including whether he is already on probation or under a suspended sentence for a previous offence. The document containing his criminal record will also give brief details of his education, employment and home circumstances – 'evidence of character', as it is called. John Smith has one previous motoring conviction, for speeding. He was fined £25 and his licence was endorsed.

Sometimes there is a strange ceremony in which the accused asks the court to 'take into consideration' other offences which he has committed similar to the one for which he is being sentenced. This device aims at achieving two ends. It enables an accused to wipe the slate clean – a sort of criminal confessional. If the court agrees to take the offences into consideration, it means that he is unlikely to be prosecuted for them in the future. It also allows the police to clear up more unsolved crimes: the carrot to the accused is that if he admits to all his offences, even those he has not been charged with, he is unlikely to get a higher sentence. Critics say that 't.i.c.'s, as they are known, are subject to abuse and a means by which the police can artificially boost their clear-up rate. There is some truth in the criticism – some defendants confess to crimes they haven't committed to get on the right side of the police – but it is difficult to assess how much.

Next, a social inquiry report is usually submitted. This is a comprehensive inquiry, prepared by a probation officer, on the defendant's background, family, home circumstances, relationships, attitudes, job situation and prospects. The report is based on interviews with the accused and those who know him well. If the accused has pleaded guilty, he may have explained his motives to the probation officer. The report usually concludes with the probation officer's opinion on the subject's suitability or otherwise for a non-prison sentence. It may suggest, for instance, that he would respond positively to probation or community service, or it may conclude that his attitude is unlikely to make these methods successful.

If the accused has previously served a custodial sentence in prison, or other custodial institution, or even if he has been in custody on remand awaiting trial, there will probably be a report from the governor or other official on how he behaved and responded. And there will be further reports if the accused has any relevant medical or mental history.

None of this applies to John Smith. There is no real likelihood of imprisonment and his crime is not the kind which requires reports.

Finally there is the plea in mitigation, delivered by the defendant's counsel (or the defendant himself if he is unrepresented). This is the tear-jerking speech of the last act, where the accused's barrister has the chance to plead for mercy and justice, to stress that the crime was the responsibility of society and not his client; alternatively, that he was led astray by evil companions. He produces a pregnant girlfriend whom the accused wants to marry and settle down with, and who will stick by him through thick and thin, and an employer who has offered him a job and is prepared to trust him. He exaggerates the remorse felt by his client and the enthusiasm with which he will reform.

Such eloquence is not necessary in John Smith's case. What Mr Brown stresses above all is how much Smith's job depends on keeping his driving licence. For Smith it is not so much the size of the fine that concerns him, but whether or not he will be able to carry on driving. Although judges and magistrates seldom disqualify someone convicted of mere careless driving, Mr Brown is taking no chances:

MR BROWN: He's a man whose job depends very much on his being able to drive. He covers a very high annual mileage, some 40,000 miles according to my instructions. And Your Honour may think that it's very much to his credit that he has only that one endorsement on his licence. Your Honour, he's thirty-six years of age; he's been driving for many years. Your Honour may think that it would be very difficult for this man, who's been a salesman all his working life, to obtain alternative employment, were he to lose his licence. That would be the position, in my respectful submission. If he loses his licence, he loses his livelihood and you see how much his employers think of him. [A letter from Smith's employer has been handed in to the judge.] Your Honour, I hope that the court will feel that in the particular circumstances of this case, that is, not only the circumstances of the accident, but the defendant's own personal circumstances, it will not be necessary to disqualify him.

The judge now has all the information on which to base his decision. The time has come for what is for many defendants the most heart-stopping moment of all, the sentence itself. This is what the training of judges is mainly aimed at; they learn the range of sentences they can apply, and the factors they should take into account. In the majority of cases the accused will know more or less what he can expect. He will have been told by his lawyers what the maximum penalty is but also that he can expect far less than that maximum. The top of the scale would only be imposed for the most heinous possible version of the crime. The maximum for theft, for instance, is ten years' imprisonment, but only a tiny percentage would get even half that – and they would be thieves with very long records. This is typical of many categories of offence. Murder is unique in having a fixed mandatory penalty, life imprisonment, although this does not usually mean life: some murderers – the husband provoked by taunts into killing his unfaithful wife in a sudden fit of jealousy, or the mercy killer – may be released after a few years. A policeman's killer will stay in for twenty or thirty.

There is, although some judges do not like admitting it, a 'tariff' for most kinds of offence. It is not an exact number of years or an exact amount of money, but it is a range within which judges tend to stay. It is not laid down by law but is the distillation of the collective practice of the courts, supported by guidance from the Lord Chief Justice and from judgments of the Court of Appeal in cases that have come before it. So judges know that for a rape a sentence of at least five years is appropriate. If it is a gang rape, eight years is nearer the mark. Multiple rapes which terrorize the public can fetch 15 years' imprisonment. These are guidelines, and the judge will look at the actual circumstances before deciding on the exact sentence. Only if he finds highly exceptional circumstances, either in favour of or against the accused, will he normally stray from the framework laid down. If he is too lenient he will have to answer to the cry of public opinion and a possible rap over the knuckles by the Lord Chancellor, as happened to the judge who sentenced a rapist to only a £2,000 fine, but there is no appeal to a higher court against an over-lenient sentence. If the judge is too savage the Court of Appeal will in all likelihood reduce the sentence on appeal.

Similarly, tariffs are used at the other end of the criminal scale. The Magistrates' Association publishes regular guidelines on the sentences to be imposed for various motoring offences. The rule of thumb for speeding, for instance, is that the fine should be £2 for every mile an hour above the speed limit. The magistrates will deduct from, or add to, that figure, depending on the particular circumstances and the particular individual.

John Smith is sure that he will not go to prison. He expects a fine. But the important thing to him is what happens to his licence.

The judge considers the other information he has been given. He knows the accused's previous criminal record – obviously a clean sheet will incline him more favourably than a string of previous convictions, especially for similar offences. The extent of offences taken into consideration will affect his mind only slightly. He will weigh the information in the social inquiry report and other reports and assess the plea in mitigation. According to Gilbert and Sullivan's *The Mikado*, a judge's task is to let the punishment fit the crime, but nowadays this is only one aspect. The punishment (or treatment) must also fit the offender.

The judge's first important task is to decide whether or not to send the accused to prison. For the defendant this is a crucial issue. It is now generally accepted by everyone in the criminal justice system that imprisoning an offender for the first time can have drastic consequences, not just for the criminal, but for his family as well; and that the benefits to society of imposing a custodial sentence are not always clear-cut.

As a result, the law tells the judge to impose imprisonment as a last resort after he has considered but rejected all non-custodial alternatives like an absolute or conditional discharge, a fine, community service, probation or a suspended sentence of imprisonment.

If a judge decides that there is no alternative to prison, the question is: for how long? Apart from the tariff and the factors particular to the individual, the judge must also consider his public duty. Is it the sort of crime that needs a long period of custody to protect the public from the offender, even if there are mitigating personal factors? Is a deterrent sentence necessary, aimed not so much at the defendant himself but at others who might be tempted to commit similar offences? Criminologists have argued mightily over whether or not deterrent sentences have any effect. The stiff sentences passed on whites found guilty of beating up blacks in Notting Hill in 1958 are believed to have had immediate deterrent effect, but the generality of the proposition is not universally accepted.

The judge must also bear in mind guidance from Lord Lane, the Lord Chief Justice, backed by the Lord Chancellor, the Home Secretary and many others, to consider passing shorter rather than longer sentences on a wide range of offenders. Such a policy would not apply to criminals convicted of offences involving violence, or to others who are a real menace to society. It has come to be realized, however, that for many offenders, especially first-timers, the main effect of imprisonment is often achieved in the initial stages of the sentence. A much longer term is counter-productive. It only accustoms the prisoner to incarceration, and hardens and embitters him. A one-month sentence can be more effective than three months, and, further up the scale, twelve months can be as productive as eighteen months or two years.

For John Smith the moment has come. The sentence is pronounced, usually with a few accompanying remarks revealing the main factors which weighed in the judge's mind. But the judge rarely gives elaborate reasons, and often he will say very little. In John Smith's case he has only this to say:

JUDGE: This case can be summed up, as far as you're concerned, that on that unfortunate day, you deliberately drove at a greatly excessive speed and you were therefore quite unable to

control your vehicle in an emergency, whether there was a
motor cycle there or not.

But for Smith, the important words are these:

> In order to relieve your worries, may I say at once that I don't
> intend to disqualify you from driving, having regard to what
> Mr Brown has ably said on your behalf. This case is going to be
> met with a fine, and the fine in your case will be one of £150.

His licence is endorsed and he is ordered to pay £150 contribution
towards his legal costs.

The trial is over. If the accused has been sentenced to
imprisonment, he descends for the last time from the dock to the cells
below, there to wait to be taken to start his period of imprisonment.
If he has been in custody during the trial, even if he is not given a
sentence of imprisonment, or even if he is acquitted, he will probably
have to go down anyway, to go through the formalities of release.
John Smith has no such formalities to go through. He can leave the
court immediately. Within minutes the courtroom is empty.

## Main types of sentence

ABSOLUTE DISCHARGE: No financial penalty, no conditions.

CONDITIONAL DISCHARGE: No financial penalty, but if offender
commits similar crime in stated period (twelve months, say)
can be brought back and given a more severe sentence for the
original offence.

FINE: Up to £2,000 at magistrates' court, unlimited in the Crown
Court.

PROBATION ORDER: Offender placed under the supervision of a
probation officer for specified period (often one or two years).
Has to have regular contact with him. Other conditions can be
attached, such as that offender must take medical treatment.

COMMUNITY SERVICE ORDER: Expressed in hours (between forty
and 240). Offender carries out socially useful tasks, such as
helping with the disabled, or decorating elderly people's
houses, at weekends and other spare time.

SUSPENDED SENTENCE OF IMPRISONMENT: For example 'nine
months suspended for two years'. If offender commits another
offence within the stated period, the original sentence can (at
the discretion of judge or magistrate) be activated, and he can
be made to serve it after any sentence imposed for the
subsequent offence.

PARTLY SUSPENDED SENTENCE OF IMPRISONMENT: For example 'twelve months imprisonment, six months suspended for two years'. Offender serves some of the sentence immediately. On release, the other part hangs over him like a suspended sentence.

IMPRISONMENT: Offender goes to prison. Usual remission is one-third of the sentence.

The range of sentences for young offenders (under twenty-one) is slightly different. Youth custody is available for offenders aged fifteen to twenty, usually for periods of more than four months. Young male delinquents between fourteen and twenty-one can be sent to a detention centre for between three weeks and four months, to undergo a 'short, sharp, shock'. Other sentences include a fine (which can sometimes be ordered to be paid by the parent); a supervision order, like an adult's probation order; and an attendance centre order – the young offender spends up to twenty-four hours, often on successive Saturday afternoons, doing brisk exercises and getting instruction in recreational activities.

## Plea-bargaining

An accused has the right to change his plea from not guilty to guilty whenever he wants, before or even during his trial. He may do so, often on the advice of his lawyer, because it is generally true that the sentence will be lower on a guilty plea than if he fights the case to the end and is convicted. The judge gives a 'discount' for the fact that the accused saved the court's time (and public money) and spared witnesses from having to give evidence. Sometimes an accused will change his plea because of a bargain struck between the defence and prosecution barristers, often with the approval of the judge. Where, for instance, there are alternative charges against the accused, one more serious than the other (murder and manslaughter, or assault occasioning grievous bodily harm and common assault are examples) the prosecution may offer to drop the more serious charge if the accused pleads guilty to the lesser.

Even where there is only one charge, the judge sometimes lets it be known, informally, to the defence barrister, that if the defendant changes his plea to guilty, he will not pass a sentence of imprisonment. The judge will not specifically say that he will definitely imprison the defendant if he persists in pleading not guilty and is convicted, but the implication is well understood.

The advantage of plea-bargaining is that the accused (assuming he is guilty) can minimize the sentence, the prosecution still get their conviction, and cases take far less time. It is clearly also an advantage to know what is in the judge's mind. Critics of plea-bargaining point to the risk that the accused is put under great pressure to plead guilty to a charge that he really wants to fight. There have been cases of innocent defendants pleading guilty to get the case over with, once the threat of imprisonment has been removed by the plea bargain. The Court of Appeal has laid down that the accused must remain free to make up his own mind, but he sometimes finds it difficult to resist his own counsel's offer. The pressure on him is the stronger because he is in the dark about what actually takes place between the judge and the barristers. The accused himself, the subject of the bargain, is excluded from the negotiations about it.

## TRIALS IN MAGISTRATES' COURTS

Why do some defendants choose trial by jury rather than by the justices? First, it is generally believed that a jury is more likely to acquit than magistrates, especially in motoring cases. Most members of a jury know that they have themselves committed the odd motoring offence. They can identify with a defendant and are likely to be more sympathetic to his defence. Magistrates claim that their higher conviction rate means only that they are less gullible. They vehemently reject the implication that they convict more innocent people. They do not mind agreeing that they may convict a larger proportion of guilty offenders than juries do. Second, a defendant will not necessarily get legal aid for a lawyer to defend him in the magistrates' court – many, though not all, lower courts are very reluctant to give legal aid in motoring cases, while virtually all defendants pleading not guilty in the Crown Court, whatever they are charged with, are likely to get legal aid. Magistrates are much more stingy.

A third reason for going to the Crown Court is that if any legal issues are involved, on the admissibility of evidence for instance, a judge is more likely to deal with them expertly and correctly than magistrates, even with the help of their clerk. Fourth and not least, at the Crown Court the defence is entitled to more advance information about the prosecution's case than at the magistrates' court. In the higher court the prosecution are obliged to disclose to the defence statements made by their witnesses, which makes it difficult for them to spring a surprise. In the magistrates courts, advance information of the details of the prosecution case is only available to defendants faced with a choice of a jury trial in the Crown Court or a summary trial before magistrates.

There are a number of advantages of trial by magistrates. First, cases do not take as long to come to trial – the average delay is less than three months compared with nine months or more in the Crown Court (though these averages conceal wide variations around the country). Waiting for trial creates understandable tensions and anxieties, and many defendants want nothing more than to have the case behind them as soon as possible. Second, cases themselves take less time. Third, the atmosphere in a magistrates' court is far less intimidating than in a Crown Court. Finally, though importantly, magistrates' justice is far cheaper. A one-day trial in a magistrates' court, with a barrister, might cost perhaps a total of £300; at the Crown Court the trial would take two days and cost nearer £1,000 (including the cost of committal proceedings), and even if the defendant is legally aided he may still find himself paying more out of his own pocket for trial in the Crown Court.

The object of the trial in the magistrates' court is exactly the same as in the Crown Court: to reach a verdict of guilty or not guilty and, if the result is a conviction, to pass sentence on the offender. The burden of proof on the prosecution and the rules of evidence apply equally to both kinds of court. The procedure, too, is broadly the same. But the absence of the jury and the relative triviality of the charges in the magistrates' court make a considerable difference to the spectacle. Instead of a bewigged judge in colourful robes sitting in solitary splendour, there are three ordinary-looking men and women wearing their ordinary clothes, neither wigged nor gowned. The lawyers, too, are dressed in everyday apparel.

The magistrates have the function of both judge and jury. They control the case, rule on points of law (with the help of their clerk), reach a decision and pass sentence. The trial follows the same path as its Crown Court equivalent. After the charge and the plea of not guilty, the prosecutor makes an opening speech, though it is addressed of course to the magistrates and not to a jury. He examines the witnesses, who are then re-examined by the defence. At the end of the prosecution case, the defence lawyer has the chance to make his submission that there is no case to answer. If that fails, he calls his witnesses, usually including the accused, who are in turn cross-examined by the prosecution. In the magistrates' court the prosecution do not always have a second, closing, speech. The defence do, however, address the magistrates at the end of their case. There is of course no equivalent of the judge's summing-up.

A magistrates' decision need not be unanimous – a two to one majority will do. Some stipendiary magistrates give reasons for their findings, but lay justices rarely do, an omission which has been the subject of criticism. Perhaps they are bearing in mind the advice of Lord Mansfield, a former Lord Chief Justice: 'Consider what you think justice requires and decide accordingly. But never give your reasons; for your judgment will probably be right but your reasons will certainly be wrong.' If the magistrates convict, the procedure for sentencing is much the same as in a Crown Court, though the magistrates will usually have social inquiry reports only in cases where the convicted defendant faces possible imprisonment, or where juveniles are involved.

# APPEALS

It is inevitable that the two and a half million criminal cases a year in England and Wales should lead to a burning sense of injustice in a few thousand hearts. Some cope with it by trying to put it behind them, forgetting the ghastly experience rather than allowing it to continue to dominate their lives. For others, the system of appeals offers some, though not perfect, relief from what they regard as injustice.

There are two main springboards for appeal: the conviction and the sentence. The two are fundamentally different. In the first the appellant claims that the result was wrong, that he was innocent of the crime of which he was found guilty. (The prosecutor cannot appeal against an acquittal.) If his contention is right, and if it is true of many convicted defendants, then it is a large blot on our system of justice, quite apart from the incalculable effect that every individual injustice has on its victim. Of course there are degrees – a conviction for overstaying a parking meter when in fact the meter was jammed is unjust, but quickly forgotten; at the other extreme there are men who have spent many years in prison for crimes they have not committed, and there have in the past been men such as Timothy Evans who were hanged and later found to be innocent.

The second kind of appeal, against sentence, has a different basis: 'I did it, but I didn't deserve such a severe sentence.' The injustice is there, but it is of a different kind.

Our system of appeals is deficient in one important respect, which is unfortunately a necessary corollary of our trial system. Magistrates very seldom give any reasons when they decide to convict a defendant. Nor do a jury when delivering their guilty verdict. We are not told, although of course we can often infer, why the decision was guilty or not guilty. Magistrates and juries do not reveal that they believed that witness or disbelieved this alibi, or thought the defendant was shifty in the witness box. So appeals have to be founded on other grounds.

Appeals against convictions by magistrates are in the form of a complete re-hearing of the case before a Crown Court judge, sitting with magistrates. The witnesses appear again and give their evidence again and the judge and justices then make up their minds according to the evidence they have heard. Where a point of law, rather than a difference about the facts, is involved there is also a form of appeal directly from magistrates' courts to the Queen's Bench Divisional Court. Appeals against magistrates' sentences also go to a Crown Court judge, sitting with magistrates.

A jury's verdict is more difficult to appeal against. They have left no clue as to their reasons. So the appeal against conviction – which goes to the Court of Appeal's Criminal Division – has to be based on other factors, for instance that there was an irregularity in the trial (in a recent case the judge pressured a jury into reaching a premature verdict), or that the judge wrongly directed the jury in his summing-up, or made a wrong legal decision during the trial (like allowing inadmissible evidence).

Over the years, the Court of Appeal has been criticized for failing to correct cases of apparent miscarriage of justice by taking an unduly restrictive view of its role and placing, in practice, far too great a burden on the appellant to prove his innocence. In particular, the court has been attacked for being loath to accept that evidence unearthed since the trial might have influenced the jury towards acquittal if they had heard it. The appellant is also at a disadvantage because the court will not interfere with a guilty verdict on the grounds that his lawyer handled the case badly, or used wrong tactics. So if his counsel didn't, for tactical reasons, call a particular witness for the defence who could have been called, the accused is stuck with that decision. There is also an unfortunate grey area between the functions of the Home Secretary, who can release prisoners before their sentence is up and grant free pardons if convinced of their innocence, and the Court of Appeal with its different standards and procedures. Prisoners claiming their innocence can be shuttled between the two, gaining satisfaction from neither. Recently, in the light of a number of cases of alleged miscarriage, there have been calls for a new body, or new procedures, to allow another look at questionable verdicts without the straitjacket of the present stringent criteria laid down by the appeal court.

It is also injustice when guilty criminals go free, and there has been concern that the law doesn't permit the re-trial of convicted defendants who have been let off on appeal because of a technicality, even where the evidence against them is very strong. Many other countries take the view that a defendant in that position ought not to be able to escape justice scot free, and they allow him to be tried again.

Winning an appeal against sentence is not easy either. It is not enough that the appeal judges would have imposed a lower sentence. They have to be convinced that the sentence actually imposed was unreasonably high. It used to be possible for appeal judges to increase the trial judge's sentence. Happily for appellants, they no longer have that power.

Some appeals arising from criminal trials will go to the House of Lords, but only if they involve important legal points. The kind of issues that the law lords have tackled in recent years include: is the intent to blaspheme necessary for the crime of blasphemy? What is the difference in law between recklessness and carelessness?

Finally, the Attorney-General is entitled to refer points of law to the Court of Appeal for clarification, even if the accused has been acquitted. The decisions in such cases do not affect the accused. An acquittal is not changed into a conviction if the Attorney-General's point is ruled valid.

## ADVERSARIAL v. INQUISITORIAL

In the English adversarial, or accusatorial, system of trial, the day of the trial is crucial. This is when the two contestants, their training and preparation completed, climb into the ring. The result is always in doubt. One of the combatants may be favourite – it may seem like an open-and-shut case for the prosecution – but there is always the chance of an upset. Nothing can be taken for granted. No doubt such a system can produce tension, but does it deliver justice? In particular, does our trial system get at the truth? Or is it so much of a tactical game that sometimes truth and justice take second place?

In the English system the police and the prosecution build up a case against the accused. It is then left to the defence to demolish it. At no stage before the trial does any independent mind look at the case as a whole. All depends on what happens in court and sometimes important witnesses, who could give vital evidence, are not heard by the jury at all.

In 1974 Luke Dougherty was accused of theft. His defence was that on the day he was alleged to have committed the crime, he was miles away on a charabanc outing, in the company of some twenty other people. His lawyers interviewed a few of the people on the charabanc, and called two of them, but they were not convincing in the witness box. An application to call some of the others was refused by the judge. Dougherty was convicted on the identification evidence of two shop assistants. After he had spent nine months in prison it was conclusively proved that his story was true after all, and he was immediately released. Under some foreign systems of law he would never have gone to prison in the first place because his charabanc trip alibi would have been thoroughly investigated. In England it is left to the defence to make their own inquiries to find witnesses, or to back up the accused's alibi. Whether they succeed is often determined by luck and the tenacity of the defendant's solicitor.

Another aspect of the adversarial system is that – much as one would like to think that justice always triumphs – court battles can be won or lost by advocacy. A good barrister, both by his skill at questioning and cross-examination, and by his speeches to the jury, can sometimes turn a losing case into a 50/50 hope, and a finely balanced one into a winner. Juries are not as susceptible to flowing oratory and appeals to emotion as they used to be, and such tactics today could even prove counter-productive. But it is only human nature to be impressed by good advocacy. The former appeal court judge Sir Sebag Shaw, a practitioner and judge of vast experience, admits he has known cases where advocacy has made a difference to the result:

> Oh yes. Notwithstanding the fact that in the end it's the judge's summing up which may have some influence upon a jury, I think if the jury's minds are prepared for whatever the judge may say by the way the case has developed in the hands of the advocate, the impression which he leaves with them may be the one which survives and persists in the end.

But only in a very small percentage of trials does the outcome depend on the efficiency and ability of the advocate, he believes.

Few lawyers and judges deny the possibility that innocent men have been sent to prison because their advocates failed to rise to the occasion, and that criminals are walking free because of the excellence of their lawyers' presentation. Is it justice that the result of a trial should hinge purely on one side's having a better advocate than the other? Perhaps not, though it is probably inevitable under our system where so much depends on what happens in court.

Tom Sargant, for twenty-five years secretary of the reform group Justice, has spent much of his life investigating cases of alleged miscarriage of justice. He points to another aspect of the adversarial system which gives him cause for concern – the method of questioning witnesses:

> I've always felt that it was not a good thing to examine witnesses on a tight rein. They're told that they must only answer the questions put to them by counsel, and they're sometimes sternly reminded of this by the judge. This means that they can fail to bring out a vital fact within their knowledge. I personally regard this as perjury by omission. In other words the jury is misled. It's not the fault of the witness, it's the fault of counsel. It really makes nonsense of our oath ... I always thought that our oath should read, I swear to tell as much of the truth as the court will allow me to.

Tom Sargant also has reservations about the technique of cross-examination:

> I've also felt that the cross-examination of witnesses, in the rather hostile and bullying way it's now done, also may not on some occasions be the best way of getting at the truth. An experienced witness, an experienced police officer or an experienced hardened criminal can

normally survive a fierce cross-examination without going under, so to speak, or being caught out. But this is just not true of a young and inexperienced witness. I just do not believe that this is the best way of getting the truth out of the witnesses that come to court. And what is more, I think the fear of the bullying treatment they might expect to receive must deter very many potential and valuable witnesses from coming to court. And because of this, the course of justice could be perverted.

All these are question marks against the adversarial system. The alternative is the inquisitorial, which most other European countries have in one form or another. The details vary from country to country, but the French example demonstrates the essential elements of the system.

Far more investigations and inquiries are carried out before the trial so that not as much depends on what happens at the trial itself. Under the French system, when a serious crime is committed, an examining magistrate (*juge d'instruction*) is appointed to look into it. He is a professional judge, usually relatively junior, whose job it is to decide whether a particular accused should be prosecuted. The strength of the French system lies in the thoroughness of the investigation of the crime, with the examining magistrate in overall control. His job is to find out as much as possible about the circumstances and background of the crime and of the person suspected of it. He is responsible for the police conduct of the investigation, and has the power himself to interrogate anyone whom he thinks can throw any light on the crime, including the suspect and any witnesses. He can even hold confrontations between the accused and witnesses. He arranges for all the necessary medical and psychiatric examinations of the accused, and all inquiries into his background. Eventually a full dossier is built up and the *juge d'instruction* is in a position to decide whether or not the prosecution should go ahead and on what charges. After making his recommendation he drops out of the picture, and the case proceeds to trial, or the accused is set free.

The system is designed to uncover the truth by pre-trial inquisition, and the French examining magistrate's task is to get at the truth. It is as much his duty to find factors pointing to innocence as to seek out evidence of guilt. Under the French system there is little doubt that everyone on the charabanc on which Luke Dougherty alleged he was travelling would have been interviewed and his case would probably never have come to trial at all.

There is a common belief that in France an accused is presumed guilty until proved innocent. That is untrue and misleading. What is true, however, is that because so much is done before trial to find out the truth, those who eventually appear before a court are more likely to be convicted, because inquiries have been so much more thorough than their English equivalent. <u>In France more than 90 per cent of those accused of serious crimes are convicted. In England the figure is only 50 per cent</u>. But under the French system many are released at an early stage who in England would have to go through the trauma of a trial.

Which is the better system, the gladiatorial, allowing the two sides to choose their weapons, or the inexorably truth-finding inquisitorial? Sir Sebag Shaw:

> If one is looking for a system which will unravel the facts, albeit ruthlessly, and present them in their worst light, then the inquisitorial system is the one which ought to be adopted. There's no doubt it would bring about more convictions. But it would put more innocent people in peril as well. And the justified boast of our adversarial system, of our English system, is that it reduces the perils of wrong convictions.

A French *avocat* – the nearest equivalent to a barrister – agrees:

> I would say that there are probably more wrongful acquittals in England than there are in France, and there may be more wrongful decisions of guilt in France, although I don't believe that there are so many unjustified decisions as some people tend to say.

## THE SCOTTISH PROCURATOR FISCAL

The Scottish system is often described as a half-way house between the English adversarial and the continental inquisitorial. In Scotland, too, a case like Luke Dougherty's would probably not have come to trial. The central figure is the Procurator Fiscal, a legally qualified civil servant, who acts as an intermediary filter between the police investigation 'and the trial. It is his decision – and not that of the police – whether to bring a prosecution or not. The police conduct the investigation and bring the initial charge against the accused. The statements of witnesses and other documents then go to the Procurator Fiscal. In the vast majority of less serious cases, he will merely endorse the police's decision as a matter of routine. In more serious cases, however, especially those that might go for trial by jury, he is more likely to use two important powers. First, because he is in ultimate charge of the investigation of crime, he can call on the police to carry out further inquiries, either to clarify points that are unclear or to try to get stronger evidence. Second, he can examine witnesses for himself (apart from the accused). The witnesses will already have given statements to the police, but seeing them in person will give the Fiscal a better idea of the strength of the evidence. The Scottish system weeds out many prosecutions which, under the English system as it used to be, would probably have gone ahead. It remains to be seen whether, under the new Crown Prosecution system in England, fewer dud cases will get to trial.

# CHAPTER VII

# THE CIVIL PROCESS

The accident in which John Smith knocked down Anne Jones in his car has had dramatic consequences for both of them. Smith has had to face a criminal court. And, through no fault of her own, Anne Jones has suffered an injury. The accident has changed her life, not only causing continuing pain, but reducing her standard of living. Does the law offer her a remedy? Can someone be made to pay?

## TYPES OF CLAIM

John Smith has been prosecuted and found guilty by a criminal court. Careless driving is a crime for which the state can levy a punishment – in John Smith's case, a fine. But in injuring Anne Jones he may also have committed a 'tort' – a civil wrong which injures someone or harms a person's property or reputation. If Anne Jones can prove that John Smith committed a tort against her – or if he admits it – she can claim compensation from him in the civil courts.

The tort involved in this case is negligence. Anne Jones will claim that John Smith caused her injury by failing to take the sort of care a reasonable driver would be expected to take. Negligence can occur in many other situations as well – for example, when a hospital gives a patient a transfusion of the wrong type of blood, or a solicitor gives his client wrong advice because he has overlooked a new law, or a company fails to make sure its employees' working conditions are safe, or a council fails to repair a loose paving stone. Anybody who is injured or who suffers financial loss through someone else's negligence has a right to sue in the civil courts for compensation.

Negligence is only one of a range of torts, or wrongs, for which it is possible to sue and claim damages. Other torts include assault, libel and slander (injuring someone else's reputation), and nuisance (spoiling someone else's enjoyment of his property, for example, by creating excessive noise or nasty smells). But by far the most common tort, in terms of the number of court actions started, is negligence.

Apart from tort, the other big category of civil action is for breach of contract. When two parties enter into a contract, they both agree

129

to carry out certain obligations. For instance, if a householder asks a firm of builders to do some work on his house, he agrees to pay them and they agree to do the job in a workmanlike manner. If he refuses to pay, they can sue him. He can then put in a defence alleging shoddy workmanship, if this is his reason for refusing to pay. Or if someone takes out a hire purchase agreement and doesn't pay the instalments, the finance company can sue him for breach of contract. The contract need not be in writing: an oral agreement to buy something from a shop or to do some work is just as much a contract as a document running to a dozen pages of legalese.

The great majority of actions in the civil courts are for money owed by one person to another – claims for unpaid debts, rent arrears or hire purchase payments; claims by suppliers of goods, work-men or professional people who have not been paid, or by the Inland Revenue for outstanding tax. Very few of these cases go to trial. In most of them there is nothing to argue about. The person sued usually owes the money but is in genuine financial difficulties, or simply trying to avoid payment. The writ or summons, which shows him that his creditor is serious and is not willing to write him off as a bad debt, will often produce payment without further ado, if the money is there. For most money claims, unless the debtor can show some defence within the time allowed – for example, shoddy workmanship or faulty goods – the creditor gets a judgment in his favour without any sort of hearing.

Personal injury claims, although they account for a much smaller number of actions started in the civil courts, are more likely to go to trial, because they more often involve an argument about where the blame lies, and provide more scope for disagreement over the size of the claim. In the Queen's Bench Division of the High Court, which deals with the more serious tort cases and the larger money claims – usually involving more than £5,000 – two-thirds of the nearly 3,000 cases a year which get as far as a trial are personal injury claims.

## Negligence

Anne Jones is unquestionably worse off than she was before the accident. The back pain she suffers if she sits for any length of time has made it impossible for her to continue doing her previous job. She has had to take a less demanding, less well-paid job. She still suffers from headaches.

Yet Anne Jones is lucky. There is someone she can clearly point to as the author of her misfortune – John Smith, already branded as a careless driver by a criminal court. Getting compensation through the courts depends on pinning the blame on someone else. But some accidents are really nobody's fault. In one freak car crash the driver died of a heart attack seconds before his car collided with a motor cycle. Because it wasn't the driver's fault, the motor cyclist, who was seriously injured, got no compensation. Sometimes accident victims fail in their claims because they were entirely to blame for their own injuries. Anne Jones is fortunate not to have to prove that John Smith was negligent. The fact that he was convicted of careless driving has really established the point for her.

If John Smith had been acquitted by the jury, it would not have spoiled Anne's chances of claiming entirely, but it would have made it more difficult. It is quite possible for someone to be acquitted of a criminal charge and still be found negligent by a civil court. This is because the standard of proof is stricter in criminal cases. A jury or magistrates will only convict someone if they are sure beyond all reasonable doubt that he committed the crime, but in a civil case the judge only has to decide whose evidence is right 'on a balance of probabilities'. In other words, in Anne Jones' case against John Smith, which is more probable: that he was negligent or that he was not?

Proving negligence can be one of the biggest hurdles for accident victims. Sometimes there is no real evidence one way or the other. There may have been no witnesses to the accident. Cases like these are very much a legal lottery. As Lord Denning put it in *What Next in the Law* (Butterworths, 1982):

> When a person is injured or killed in a road accident, the law always was – and still is – loaded heavily against him. It is because the burden is on him to prove that the defendant was negligent. If he leaves the matter in doubt – so that it is uncertain whether the defendant was negligent or not – the plaintiff suffers.

In one case, a seven-year-old boy was struck by a car while riding his bicycle, and suffered brain damage. The High Court awarded him £40,000. But the Court of Appeal set the award aside, ruling that no negligence had been proved. A further appeal by the boy's father to the House of Lords was unsuccessful.

The law can be very unfair. Suppose three men are crippled as the result of three different accidents. The first has an accident at work, the second is hit by a car, and the third damaged during surgery. Their relative chances of winning compensation through the courts are widely different. The work accident victim is best off. Employers have a number of special duties laid down by Parliament – for example, to fence dangerous machinery. If they break any of these duties, an injured employee is entitled to compensation without proving negligence. In many cases, a worker will be able to sue his employers for negligence as well, giving him two bites at the cherry. The road accident victim can only rely on negligence, and this is sometimes hard to prove. But in medical mishaps, proving fault is much more difficult. Many road accidents are caused by drivers who take obvious risks – drunk drivers, for example. With doctors, there are many more cases on the borderline between negligence and mere error of judgement. The difficulty of deciding on which side of the borderline a doctor's action falls is illustrated by the case of a handicapped baby, Stuart Whitehouse. Stuart was born with severe brain damage. His mother said the doctor had pulled too long and hard on the forceps. She sued the doctor and the hospital and won £100,000 in the High Court. But the Court of Appeal reversed the decision. The doctor's use of the forceps did not amount to negligence, said the judges. It was simply an error of judgement, such as any competent doctor could have made. The House of Lords agreed. So the baby's parents got no compensation. Only about one-third of the medical negligence claims are successful compared with an overall success rate for personal injury claims of 86 per cent, according to the 1978 report of the Royal Commission on Civil Liability and Compensation for Personal Injury (the Pearson Commission).

Despite the high success rate, comparatively few accident victims make claims, for reasons discussed in Chapter I: lack of awareness of their rights, fear of the cost, not knowing how to go about it. High on the list of deterrents is fear of going to court – most people wrongly expect actually to have to appear in court to get compensation. The reality is that only one in a hundred personal injury claims started ever gets to court, and around one-third of those that do are settled at the door of the court without a trial. According to the British Insurance Association, the vast majority of successful claims are settled before a writ has even been issued.

## STARTING THE ACTION

Anne Jones goes to see her solicitor, Mr Long, who dealt with her divorce a few years before. He is the only solicitor she knows.

He reassures her on two main concerns: first, on her income, she will certainly be eligible for legal aid. Second, the fact that Smith was found guilty of careless driving, even though acquitted of reckless driving, is very much in her favour. He tells her that there should be no difficulty in proving that he was negligent and therefore she should be able to recover compensation – damages – against him. The only question is, how much? Her solicitor asks her the details of the accident and her injuries. She tells him that since the accident she has suffered from persistent headaches and bad back trouble. One wrist was broken and is still stiff. As a result of all this, she has found herself unable to go back to her old job as a senior secretary because she can no longer use a typewriter comfortably, and her backache makes it difficult to sit for long periods. She has been forced to take on very junior unrewarding work as a general office girl: filing, making tea, and doing other menial jobs. Mr Long asks her in detail about her finances, so that he can apply for legal aid on her behalf, and also to give him some idea of the amount to claim.

Anne Jones leaves her solicitor's office an hour later. She has embarked on a long and difficult journey through the legal system.

The solicitor now takes over. John Smith was insured and her claim will in effect be against his insurance company. Although the legal proceedings will still be against Smith, in practice he fades out of the picture and the insurers take all the decisions. Most successful negligence claims are covered by insurance. Drivers have to insure against causing harm to other road users and employers must insure against injury to their employees. Most businesses carry public liability insurance, to cover claims by customers or anyone else injured in the course of their business activities. Many householders are covered against injury to tradesmen and visitors. Since the insurance company's money is at stake, it takes over complete control of the action as soon as it is notified of a claim. The person claiming compensation is put at an immediate disadvantage. The insurance company's solicitors are specialists, with considerable skill and experience in dealing with negligence cases. Tactical skills are arguably more important than knowing the law, and they only come with dealing with cases in volume. Victims are less likely to have a specialist lawyer, simply because they are unlikely to know how to find one. Anne Jones is lucky. Her solicitor Mr Long has had a good deal of experience in this field.

Solicitors do not act uniformly in pursuing a claim on behalf of a client. Some will start legal proceedings immediately, by issuing a writ, and then start negotiations with the other side to see if an early settlement of the claim is possible. Others may have extensive discussions with the insurance company in the hope that the claim can be settled even before a writ needs to be issued. Whatever tactics they use, it is a fact that the vast majority of accident claims are settled with the insurers within a few months.

As soon as he knows that Anne Jones as been granted legal aid, Mr Long issues a writ. Issuing a writ straight away has two advantages. If the insurance company admits John Smith was at fault, Anne Jones will be able to apply to have some of the money early – as an interim payment – while the haggling goes on about the final settlement. And she will be able to claim interest on the full amount from the date the writ was issued. Mr Long thinks there is a reasonable chance of an early settlement, especially as there appears to be little doubt about Smith's negligence. The only issue is likely to be how much Anne Jones gets for her injuries. To determine that, it is necessary for her to undergo a medical examination by an expert. The solicitor arranges for her to see Mr Collins, a consultant orthopaedic surgeon.

Mr Collins' report mentions that Anne Jones had a history of recurrent attacks of back pain since childhood. He concludes:

It is now sixteen months since this accident and it appears that this girl is now left with permanent stiffness of her dominant right wrist which will cause her considerable difficulty doing all kinds of daily activities for the foreseeable future. It appears doubtful at the present time whether she will be able to return to her previous occupation as a senior secretary because of the persistent symptoms in her wrist and back and her persistent headaches.

Her persistent back symptoms prevent her from sitting in one position for any length of time, and in particular it seems that she is unable to sit at her typewriter for any length of time. Her persistent headaches prevent her concentrating and she still has to lie down at times during the day. She still requires analgesic tablets.

In conclusion this girl has not fully recovered from her injuries, and it seems that she may well in fact never do so. It is unlikely that she will ever return to her previous occupation as a senior secretary, and may have to be content with her present, considerably less demanding, job. Although some improvement may yet take place, it is unlikely that this will be significant.

For all practical purposes, therefore, her present situation can be taken as permanent.

Again, it is a question of tactics when to let the other side see the medical report. Mr Long sends this report to the insurance company immediately, but they want to arrange for Anne Jones to see their own consultant orthopaedic surgeon, Mr Longfield. His report is very different and much more sceptical. He says, for instance, that although six months after the accident the hospital noted her to be fit for work and discharged her: '. . . it appears that she did not immediately return to full-time work.' He puts far greater emphasis on her previous back pains than did Mr Collins. Mr Longfield concludes:

It was my general assessment with this patient that she was of a rather highly-strung and nervous temperament, possessing a somewhat low pain threshold. In my opinion the stiffness in her wrist has persisted for this length of time because she has not made any concerted effort to use the wrist normally. I see no reason why she is not able to type relatively normally.

In my opinion the injury to the back has been an exacerbation of the previous back weakness. When I questioned her closely on the severity of her back symptoms, she admitted to me that her symptoms now were not significantly different to her symptoms prior to the accident, and this is confirmed by the relative absence of physical findings on clinical examination today. Mrs Jones finds herself in a somewhat unfortunate situation having to live on her own and support, unaided, a child, and it would seem to me that the strain of these responsibilities has been rather much for her and has adversely affected her ability to recover from what were, in fact, relatively mild injuries.

Her persistent headaches are, in my opinion, not post-concussional and are more likely psychological in origin, precipitated by her unfortunate situation.

With regard to her ability to work, it is my assessment that there is no reason for her not being able to return to her previous occupation immediately, and in my view, and apparently in the view of the doctors at the hospital who were looking after her, she was able physically to return to such work about six months after this accident.

If the two medical reports had agreed about her injuries and their continuing effect, the insurance company and Anne Jones' solicitor would almost certainly have reached agreement on a figure, after a period of bargaining. But the two experienced doctors disagree and no settlement is possible. The two sides are many thousands of pounds apart in their assessments of what the claim is worth. Anne Jones' solicitor has no alternative but to continue formal legal proceedings. And so begins a highly complex game of negotiation, barter and bluff.

## DAMAGES

Anne Jones' claim is for damages for personal injuries sustained in a car accident. Damages vary widely depending on the kind of civil claim. Damages for breach of contract, for instance, are calculated differently from damages for libel, or for personal injury. What lies at the heart of all claims for damages is compensation – the law tries to compensate a plaintiff for a wrong done to him. Sometimes it is easy to work out how much the damages should be: if a shopkeeper sells something for an agreed sum of £100 and he is not paid, he sues the buyer for £100, and that is what he will get if he wins. But sometimes it is much more difficult. How much should a negligent motorist have to pay for knocking down a pedestrian and breaking his leg or skull? And how much is a person's reputation worth if a newspaper falsely tells the world that he is a crook?

There are broadly two categories (or heads as they are called) of damages: the direct financial loss on which a precise figure can be placed, and the more nebulous, less easy to quantify, compensation for pain and suffering, loss of future earnings, and other future losses. Anne Jones will be entitled, first, to money she has actually spent: medical and nursing bills, or damaged clothing, for instance, as well as lost earnings – most employers will carry a sick employee for a few weeks but can rarely keep him or her on full pay for months. These quantifiable amounts are called 'special damages'. Usually they are agreed between the two sides, as in Anne Jones' case.

The disputes usually concern the other head, 'general damages' – the less precise items. Anne Jones is claiming for pain and suffering, both past and future. Her wrist was broken, her back injured and she gets headaches which may go on for some time. Her injuries could have been much more serious. She could have been disfigured or disabled, in which case she would have been entitled to very much larger sums of compensation. In some cases damages are given for 'loss of amenity' – the inability to take part in activities previously enjoyed, like sport or dancing. It is obviously very difficult to put a precise figure on the value of particular injuries, but in practice lawyers get guidance from the awards given by judges in previous similar cases. These are collated and regularly updated in a book known as Kemp & Kemp, the bible on damages. So lawyers will know, for instance, that as a rough guide an amputated finger is worth about £3,000, and the loss of an eye around £15,000. Anne Jones is also claiming for future loss of earnings. In her case she is asking for the difference between the salary she used to get in her old job and the lower salary she is getting in the much more menial job she has to do now. For some people an accident can mean the permanent loss of promotion prospects, and for that, too, compensation is payable.

Those categories apply to damages for personal injuries. They are slightly different for other kinds of damages claims, but the way of assessing damages is similar: actual financial loss, plus compensation for more intangible results. A businessman suing for breach of contract, for instance, might claim lost future profits. In some cases it is enough just to put the plaintiff in the financial position he would have been in but for the wrong done to him. In many other categories, personal injuries being one, the law attempts the impossible task of putting a monetary value on something for which money is no real compensation.

## BEFORE THE TRIAL

Robert Alexander QC likens a civil action to a game of tennis: 'The process before you get to court is perhaps similar to the early stages in a long rally at tennis. That is, they are necessary, predictable and involve each side seeking to manoeuvre into a better position for the decisive strokes.' The rules of civil procedure in the High Court are extremely detailed and complex. It takes a book of 3,500 pages known to lawyers as 'the White Book', to explain them all. The county court, which deals with most civil actions, has a 2,000 page book of its own, 'the Green Book'.

The broad outline of every civil claim is much the same. It starts formally with the plaintiff serving a writ on the defendant, (in the county court, a summons.) Anne Jones' writ is short and just gives the bare essentials of what is being claimed – damages for personal injuries – and when the accident happened. There is time enough to fill in the details during the exchange of documents, called pleadings, that will follow. These exchanges are crucial in building up each side's case. They also allow the opponents to gain an idea of what is being claimed against them. The procedure makes it almost impossible for either side to spring a real surprise: although the identity of all the witnesses will not be revealed to the other side, exactly what is being claimed will and must be known. As the case goes on, each side will be asking questions of the other to try and find out more. For instance, they can call for 'further and better particulars' to clarify or amplify something alleged. And there is also a stage known as 'discovery', where each side allows the other to inspect the key documents in the case. The rules governing what need and need not be disclosed are elaborate. But, for instance, any reports by doctors or other experts on which either side plans to rely will have to be shown – the litigants are not allowed to keep them up their sleeves and suddenly produce them at the trial. At the end of the pleadings, the contestants in the civil trial will know quite a lot about each other's case.

## The negotiations

The aim of both sides will be to avoid going to court at all, because they both know how much legal costs escalate once the trial approaches, and how uncertain the trial result can be. So both sets of lawyers are anxious to settle if possible. Negotiations take place. There are offers and counter offers. Eventually, in most cases, the two sides reach a compromise, and the agreed sum is paid over. In more stubborn cases, something else may be needed. One of the main devices in the tactical game aimed at achieving settlement is the payment into court. It can be used in all kinds of civil cases when the amount is in dispute, not just in personal injuries claims.

### Payment into court

The payment in, as it is usually known, is a sum of money literally paid to the court by the defendants – in effect John Smith's insurance company – in final settlement of the plaintiff's claim. That triggers a legal rule aimed at putting pressure on the plaintiff. Anne Jones must decide either to take the money or to pursue the case to trial. But there is a catch: if she refuses the offer and at the end of the trial the judge awards her less – even a penny less – than the payment in, she will have to pay not only her own costs, but also those of her opponent, from the date the offer was made. It is an essential rule that the trial judge will not know the amount of the payment in, and his decision will therefore be unaffected by it. As it happens, Anne Jones is on legal aid, so she will not have to pay the other side's legal costs herself, if she fails to beat the payment in, but they will be deducted from any damages she is awarded, thus leaving her with much less. A plaintiff paying his own costs is equally at risk, and it sometimes happens that the whole award of damages is eaten up by legal costs following the rejection of a payment into court.

The offer has therefore to be calculated extremely carefully to make it tempting enough for Anne Jones to take it. The insurance company's solicitor and their claims manager hold a conference with their barrister, Mr Green, to work out the amount they will be paying into court. The defence stick by the conclusion of Mr Longfield's report that Anne Jones' injuries are not as severe as she has painted them, that they are not long-lasting and that she could go back to her old kind of job if she wanted to. They assess the general damages she would get at around £6,000–£8,000 and add the special damages (medical bills and other money already spent, and past loss of earnings) which are at the time around £4,000. Then they add a little to make the offer slightly more tempting, and also add a further amount for interest. Eventually the lawyers reach a figure of £13,500 to be paid into court.

The pressure is now on Anne Jones to respond. It is a crucial decision. Should she go on in the hope that she can get more, but take the risk that she might land up with very little once the costs have been taken care of? She needs counsel's advice on whether or not to accept. A few weeks later she goes with her solicitor to the Middle Temple chambers of Mr Grey, the barrister who has been briefed in her case.

Mr Grey has read the medical reports and notices the discrepancies between them. He needs to test the strengths and weaknesses of Anne Jones' case before reaching a conclusion. For more than an hour he questions her about every detail of her medical condition. At the end of it he is broadly satisfied that Anne Jones is being truthful, and that Mr Longfield's report is not altogether reliable. Mr Grey believes that she will get about £9,500 for pain and suffering – the headaches and the back especially. He also takes the view, contrary to that of Mr Longfield and the insurance company, that she will not be able to take on a job that pays as much as she used to get. He thinks that for at least four years she will lose £2,000 a year in salary. The four years is an arbitrary time period. It is quite low because Mr Grey thinks that she may recover from the effects of her injuries to some extent, or that her financial circumstances might change – if she remarries for instance. She is still young and attractive and this counts against her in working out her damages. He also adds £2,500 for paying someone to do the housekeeping tasks that her injuries prevent her from doing. With the special damages and interest, the total comes to £25,500 – nearly double the sum paid into court by the insurance company.

Mr Grey warns her that she will still be taking a bit of a gamble by rejecting the payment in, but:

MR GREY: In those circumstances the risk that you face, if you don't accept the money that's now paid into court, in my view, is very slight. Had they paid a sum in of say £20,000 or something of that order, I'm bound to say that my advice would be very much less confident.

ANNE JONES: I'm not really prepared to accept that amount of money. I think it is too little and it is not just that. I feel that having got this far, I want to take it all the way.

She has decided to take the risk. But should there be such a risk in the first place? Is it fair that thousands of pounds should turn on whether the judge awards a pound more or a pound less than the amount paid into court? In theory the payment-in procedure exists to discourage frivolous or speculative actions. The idea is that no one will wish to continue unless he believes he has a genuine case. It is also meant to stop plaintiffs' dragging matters out unnecessarily. But it can sometimes be used with very different ends in mind. Robert Alexander QC:

In practice it's often used, and perfectly legitimately used within the present system, by defendants to pay in the minimum possible sum they think the plaintiff might get at trial, which places the plaintiff in an unattractive position. He's really in a comparable position to someone who has two cards numbering sixteen, at vingt-et-un or blackjack, and has to decide whether to draw another card or to stick in the hope that the bank goes bust. Now while that may be all very well in a game of chance, it's not an attractive decision for a personal litigant to have to take.

A number of proposals for reform of the system have been suggested in recent years to try to take the 'all or nothing' element out of it. The Winn Committee in 1968 called it a blunt instrument which did not always serve to promote the fair settlement of disputes. A committee of the reform body Justice in 1981 said that it could also be a sharp instrument in the hands of defendants who abused the process by using it to tempt needy plaintiffs into accepting less than their fair due. The Justice committee proposed that the judge should have greater discretion about the award of costs. The parties to the litigation would continue to make offers and counter-offers but, if the case went to trial, the judge, after making his decision, would be entitled to look at all the circumstances of the negotiations and the behaviour of the parties. He would be able to assess whether one side or the other had acted unreasonably. So if he thought that a plaintiff had unreasonably refused a good offer from the defendant and instead chose to go to trial he could, even if the plaintiff won, order that he shouldn't get all the legal costs from the other side that he would normally be awarded. ·

Not all lawyers accept that reform along the lines suggested by Justice is necessary. Richard Scott, chairman of the Bar 1982-3:

> I think that the system of payment-in is essential and is necessary in order to protect defendants from being harrassed by actions which ought not to be continued . . . And although that may sometimes appear to place great stress on the plaintiff in having to decide whether to continue the case and be in danger as to costs, from the point of view of the defendant I think in many cases it would be very unjust to the defendant if he were not able to protect himself against the burden of costs by making a payment-in.

Payment into court is just one of the pressures both sides are under to settle matters out of court. In fact the great majority of civil actions are settled before trial, in both the High Court and the county court. The cost of a case that goes to trial can easily be double or treble that of a claim settled by negotiation and both sets of lawyers are well aware of this.

The pressure to settle does not, however, fall evenly on the two sides. Very often, especially in actions for personal injuries arising out of accidents, it is a fight between David and Goliath, the individual versus the big insurance company. It is equally uneven in many cases where, for instance, big stores or companies sue customers for money allegedly owing – the individual may believe he does not owe the money, or that the goods are defective, but he is often overwhelmed by the prospect of taking on the big battalions.

It is true that legal aid is on the side of David. But the legal aid fund is cautious and often less than generous. It will provide some help but will not be able to match the resources of insurance companies and other big organizations. An insurance company also has time in its favour. The individual plaintiff wants to get the whole case over with as soon as possible – not only so that he can get his hands on the money quickly, but also because of the constant stress and emotional tension that involvement in a legal action usually brings. A company feels no such pressures and it is often in its interests in borderline cases to string out the proceedings and wear down the other side.

The delays of the law are added to the tactical delays of the litigants, so that it can take several years between accident and trial. The personal strain is enormous. For an insurance company a legal claim is a matter of business; for the individual it is something whose result can affect his whole life. While the case is going on, it can dominate it. Often, of course, the legal proceedings follow another nasty experience – an accident. Many litigants succumb to the strain and give up the legal battle by withdrawing or settling on inadequate terms. Anne Jones, however, perseveres. Eventually, three years after the accident and more than two years after the writ against Smith was issued, the case is listed for trial in the High Court.

## THE DAY OF TRIAL

A little after ten o'clock in the morning Anne Jones and her solicitor arrive at the Royal Courts of Justice in the Strand in London, where about sixty courts are about to begin the day's business. They are early so that they can have a few final words with her barrister, Mr Grey, and her doctor, Mr Collins, who will be a witness about her medical condition. There is also a good chance that they will be offered more money, even at this late stage. Perhaps as many as a third of the cases that reach court are settled literally at the doors. Michael Wright QC explains:

> This is really the time when everybody begins to face up to the realities. The plaintiff, who may up to that point have been making extravagant claims for the size of his claim or the amount of money that he's lost, now realises that he has to go into the witness box, take the oath and persuade a judge of the validity of what he is saying. And it's usually at this stage that possibly an element of cold feet begins to creep into the negotiations.
>
> Equally the defendant and his advisers have to face up to the fact that their evidence may not be as strong as they hope, and they may not be able to produce so powerful a defence. The parties are there, seeing each other face to face; they are able to take immediate instructions from their clients, from their witnesses, from their experts, and make a final assessment of the strengths or weaknesses of their case.

To that can be added the fact that by this time they know who the judge is going to be, and whether he has a reputation for being stingy or generous.

A few yards away from Anne Jones and her team, in the corridor outside the courtroom where the trial is to take place, the opposing side is talking in low whispers. Mr Simms, the insurance company's solicitor, tells Mr Green, their barrister, that they are willing to raise the offer to £17,000 – £3,500 more than the amount they paid into court.

In a scene duplicated thousands of times every year outside hundreds of courtrooms, in the county courts as well as the High Court, the defendant's barrister approaches the plaintiff's to tell him of the last-minute offer aimed at avoiding a full-blown trial. Mr Green tells Mr Grey that his clients will offer £17,000 but no more. Mr Grey is certain that Anne Jones will not be interested in that figure, but he is duty bound to convey the new offer to her. Anne Jones wants to reject it and her solicitor and barrister agree. The barristers meet again and Mr Grey informs his opponent of Anne Jones' rejection. The insurance company is not prepared to go any higher, so the trial will have to go ahead.

There is no jury. The High Court judge alone will decide. In Anne Jones' case his job will be limited to only one decision – how much to award her. Because the insurance company has admitted that John Smith's driving was at fault, the judge will not have to rule on who was to blame – something which is very often in dispute. He will not even have to make up his mind on whether Anne Jones was partly to blame – guilty of contributory negligence. If all these issues were still in dispute it would have been a much longer trial. For the plaintiff, Anne Jones, witnesses would have been called to testify that John Smith was driving carelessly or recklessly; that he was going far too fast in the circumstances, so that he wasn't able to avoid hitting her. It would have been, to a large extent, a rehash of the evidence called at Smith's Crown Court trial.

The defence would have found it difficult to claim that Smith was totally faultless, but it might have argued that Anne Jones played her part in the accident by stepping off the kerb when it was not safe to do so. It would have been put to her in cross-examination that she had not looked properly to see whether there was anything coming. It is possible that, after hearing all the witnesses, the judge might have found Anne Jones guilty of some contributory negligence. This is expressed in percentage terms, so Anne Jones might have been, say, 25 per cent to blame. This would not have lost her the case altogether, but it would have reduced her damages by that percentage.

But perhaps the most important effect of fighting not only about damages but also about liability is that it adds a new dimension to the decision about whether to accept a payment into court. If there was a chance of losing the case, or having her damages reduced because of her own contributory negligence, she would obviously have been far more disposed to accept the payment into court. The result of a court case is never certain and many lawyers advise their clients to accept the bird in the hand. All this is academic in Anne Jones' case. The insurance company were faced with a verdict of guilty of careless driving against John Smith. That hardly augured well for a successful defence of the civil claim, with its easier burden of proof. The insurance company therefore decided to throw in the towel on liability and fight on 'quantum' – how much.

## THE TRIAL

The English civil trial, like its criminal counterpart, is conducted on adversarial lines. There are two contestants, each having free rein through their lawyers to run the case as they see fit, and to call or not call what witnesses they want. The judge is the sole arbiter both of fact and of law. He seldom intervenes, even if he feels that one or other side has not called a key witness. As in criminal trials, many cases are won and lost on tactics and advocacy rather than on where the truth lies.

The trial begins with the plaintiff's counsel, Mr Grey, outlining Anne Jones' case. The judge has previously read through the various documents, including the medical reports, and has some idea of what the trial is about. But he does not know that there has been a payment into court, and even if he suspects there has been one (it is relatively common practice) he does not know how much it is. Anne Jones' barrister summarizes the circumstances of the accident, and explains that the crux of the case is the disagreement between the two doctors. Her own medical expert, Mr Collins, says that she may never recover fully from the injuries she received to her wrist and back, and from her headaches. As a result she is unable to go back to her old job as a senior secretary, and has had to take on more menial work. He tells the judge that the defence doctor, Mr Longfield, believes that Anne Jones' symptoms are exaggerated, that her problems are mainly psychological and that she could return to something similar to her old work if she wanted to.

After his opening speech the first witness is called. Anne Jones herself takes the oath and embarks on what is for her a vital hour. The impression she makes on the judge is crucial. If he thinks she is telling the truth about the effect of her injuries, then the amount of damages is likely to be close to what she is hoping for. But if he believes she is exaggerating, it will affect not only the amount of damages she gets but also her costs.

How does a judge know if a witness is telling the truth? Sir George Baker, who was a judge for eighteen years, explains:

One has to remember that judges are not infallible. We haven't got a crystal ball into which we can gaze and get the answers to whether or not the witness is truthful. And I would be the first to admit I may have been led up the garden on various occasions. But having made these qualifications, I think over the years – and remember one has twenty years at the Bar probably before going on the bench – one builds up a sort of inbred sense of whether the witness is telling the truth, exaggerating, or simply telling a pack of lies. And that is quite apart from the testing of the witness's evidence against the evidence of other witnesses. And witnesses of course can be mistaken. It's more often the case that they're mistaken, or their recollection is faulty, than that they're deliberately lying. The deliberate really good liar is probably pretty difficult to detect.

Anne Jones' counsel is concerned about the suggestion in Mr Longfield's report that she has not tried very hard to overcome her injuries, and did not go back to work as soon as she could. He asks her about her first temporary job, six months after the accident.:

ANNE JONES: Well, I was sent to an office on the first day, and by lunchtime I was feeling very bad indeed. I suddenly realized that I couldn't actually sit still at a typewriter for the length of time that was needed. And the next morning if anything it was worse. It was very painful when I woke up. And I'm afraid that I had to leave that job at lunchtime. I couldn't even see the job through until the end of the day.

She sums up her symptoms as they are, three years after the accident:

The back is as bad as it was two weeks after the accident. I haven't noticed any difference, any improvement at all in the pain. My headaches are again just as bad, I get them two or three times a week since the accident. My left and right wrists are a lot better obviously. My left wrist is still a bit stiff. The right wrist, I just can't seem to carry heavy things in it, and I do have a certain amount of difficulty typing. There are just certain movements that I find rather difficult to do with my right wrist – it's just stiff.

The judge intervenes, and asks her to grip his arm, to test how hard she can grip.

At the end of Anne Jones' evidence, it is the turn of Mr Green, the defence barrister, to cross-examine. His task is to dent the good impression she seems to have made. He asks her detailed questions about how she uses her wrist, trying to show that she could type more easily than she admits. He tries to emphasize inconsistencies between what she told Mr Longfield, according to his report, and what she said in court. He probes an apparent discrepancy about her back. Mr Longfield's report said that she told him that the back pain was not very different from what it had been before the accident. If that is so, it suggests that the accident was not, or only marginally, to blame.

ANNE JONES: No, that really was a misunderstanding, because what I said to him was that the area of the pain was not any different. In other words, I was getting the pain in the same area that I used to get the pain when I was a child. And the pain was a similar sort of pain. But this is ten times worse than anything I'd had as a child.

At the end of his cross-examination of Anne Jones, the defence barrister, Mr Green, is reasonably satisfied that he has sown some doubts about her backache, which she has said is her main problem.

The only other witness for the plaintiff is Mr Collins, Anne Jones' consultant orthopaedic surgeon. He repeats more or less what he said in his report. The case has clearly come down to a straight question of Anne Jones' truthfulness. At the end of Mr Collins' evidence, the plaintiff's case is closed.

Mr Green, the barrister for the insurance company, does not need to make an opening speech: the issue is clear enough. In a more complicated case he might have given the judge a brief outline of the main points, but these speeches by counsel in a civil case are not as important as they are in criminal trials, where there is an untrained jury who have to have the case explained to them in simple terms.

The only witness for the defence is Mr Longfield. The most crucial point for the defence is his opinion of Anne Jones' back injury, which she has said was the main reason she couldn't go back to her old job. Mr Longfield repeats that he had understood from her that the back pain was much the same as she had suffered from before the accident. He accepts that the accident might have exacerbated it, but only to a mild degree. It is vital for Anne Jones' case that the judge should not believe Mr Longfield's version. Her counsel, Mr Grey, starts his cross-examination by trying to establish that the meeting between him and Anne Jones was tense and that the two did not get on very well. Mr Longfield denies this. He concedes, however, that he might have been mistaken in saying that Anne Jones had not tried to go back to work as soon as she could. This misunderstanding has an effect on the whole of the cross-examination. Mr Longfield's admission that he might have misinterpreted what she said on this point puts a question mark against the rest of his evidence.

The next important area for the defence barrister to probe concerns Anne Jones' back injury. Mr Longfield has recorded in his report that the back was no worse than before the accident. Mr Grey questions Mr Longfield.

MR GREY: In her evidence to the court, she said she certainly wasn't telling you that it was the same as the pre-accident state had been. And yet that was your impression, according to your report.

MR LONGFIELD: That was what my impression was at the time from what she told me.

MR GREY: Nonetheless, you knew that she was continuing to wear a corset, as necessary.

MR LONGFIELD: Yes.

MR GREY: Which would be inconsistent with the pre-accident condition that you would have expected her back to be in.

MR LONGFIELD: I think that certainly I would accept that she had suffered a little more back pain than she had previously. I'm prepared to accept that.

This will prove an important admission from Mr Longfield. He is the only witness for the defence. The next stage is for both counsel to make their closing speeches, which are short – the trial has lasted only a few hours and the judge, unlike a jury, needs no spoon-feeding about the crucial issues.

The defendant's counsel is first to speak. He tries to play down Mr Longfield's apparent back-tracking. He suggests also that Anne Jones' symptoms may in part be caused by worry about the litigation and will therefore disappear when the case ends.

It is also in the closing speeches that both sides outline what level of damages they think are appropriate under each heading. On future loss of earnings, the difference in salary between Anne Jones' former job and her present one, Mr Green argues that no award at all should be made, on the strength of Mr Longfield's opinion that nothing is stopping her from going back to her old job. He also says that no award should be made for housekeeping help, because she doesn't really need it. Mr Green suggests a figure of between £6,000 and £8,000 for general damages – pain and suffering. Special damages, the sum awarded for medical and other expenditure arising from the accident, are agreed at £6,951 (they have risen considerably since the payment into court).

In his speech, Mr Grey, Anne Jones' barrister, asks the judge to accept her evidence and reject Mr Longfield's findings. It is not customary for the plaintiff's counsel to ask for a precise sum of damages, but he can suggest a range: around £20,000 for loss of future earnings, which he argues could go on for many years, as could her need for housekeeping help, the cost of which he estimates at about £8,000. Pain and suffering, he suggest, should be compensated for by a payment of up to £10,000.

Both sides have now had their say. It is up to the judge to decide. Unlike juries or magistrates in a criminal case, judges in civil cases give the reasons for their decisions. The judge starts off by briefly summarizing the facts of the case. He then gives his views on the contentious areas. First he deals with the suggestion that Anne Jones hadn't tried hard enough to go back to her old job.

JUDGE: I am quite satisfied that she made the effort to get back to work, that she simply couldn't do it; and that the hospital's conclusion that she was then fit for work is something to which I ought not to have any real regard.

On the headaches, which Mr Longfield had suggested were largely psychological:

JUDGE: To say that it's psychological and arises from an accumulation of troubles, of divorce, being left with a young child, the litigation and so on, is only I think half the story, if it is half the story. The real causative factor of the headaches, it seems to me, was and still is, the head injury.

Then he comes to the crucial question of Anne Jones' back:

I think whatever one may say about the back, we always come back to the position that it wasn't troubling her before the accident, it has troubled her since, it is troubling her now, and I am bound really to accept the evidence of Mr Collins who says that there will be, in his view, a great possibility of trouble in the future.

The judge now comes to the important part of the decision: how much? For future loss of earnings, he awards £14,000. For housekeeping he gives £1,500 – because he doesn't believe Anne Jones will need help for long. For general damages, he settles on a figure of £8,500. And he awards the agreed special damages. The total comes to £30,951.

Anne Jones has done well. The damages she has been awarded are well above the final offer at the doors of the court, and more than twice the payment into court. This means that the judge orders the defendants, the insurance company, to pay her costs. Because she is on legal aid, the costs will in fact be paid by the insurance company directly to the legal aid fund which financed her case.

It is not quite finished for Anne Jones. There is still the possibility that the insurance company will appeal. There seems to be no point of law which they can contest – the case raises no legal issues. The only possible appeal is the against amount of damages. The Court of Appeal will usually only interfere with an award of damages if it is totally unreasonable, or made on the wrong legal basis. The insurance company may think that the amount Anne Jones got is too high, but it is clearly not absurdly high. They decide the chances of a successful appeal are very slim, and decide to leave matters alone.

Anne Jones' three-year legal ordeal is finally over. She has pursued her case to the bitter end. But many like her have fallen along the way, because they didn't know their rights, or they couldn't afford the cost of litigation and yet were not eligible for legal aid, or because they lacked the determination or the stamina to carry on, and accepted inadequate offers of settlement just to relieve the pressure on them. And finally there are those who overcome all the hurdles and have their trial, but lose. Robert Alexander QC sums up:

> ... whilst everyone operates it fairly and conscientiously within the rules, the rules are not satisfactory for resolving disputes. They're particularly unsatisfactory where individuals are involved as, for example, in personal injury litigation, where individuals are, as claimants, suing companies ... I think only people who've been involved in it can realise the uncertainty, the emotional energy and the anxiety that go into litigation.

## REFORM

Why should it be such a long, harrowing and costly process? The three factors are intimately linked. On the whole, the shorter the process, the cheaper and less traumatic it is.

It took Anne Jones three years to get her money. A survey carried out for the Lord Chancellor in 1985 showed that the average High Court case took more than five years to come to trial from the date of the accident. The senior partner of one of London's biggest solicitors' firms:

> I say to my client in a personal injury case, well, we've done all the intermediate work, we're now ready for a hearing. But because there's a doctor involved who has to give evidence, I have to have a fixed date. The delay in London is fifteen months. Now that's a tremendous factor in stress and strain for the individual who is sitting at home for fifteen months wondering if

he's going to get any money and if so, how much. I believe that something should be done urgently that at the end of the day will reduce these delays, which I think are totally unacceptable.

What can be done? The main attempts to speed up civil litigation have concentrated on the pre-trial stage. Often delays are the fault not of the law, but of the lawyers. Time limits are laid down by the rules for filing certain documents, but they are rarely adhered to. It is usually up to one side's solicitors to badger the opposing side and, if necessary, to go to court to get an order hurrying them up. But few solicitors like to be unpleasant to their colleagues. Even if the lawyers are keen, they may be halted in their enthusiasm by a bottleneck in the system. For instance, there are High Court officials, called Masters, who have to make various decisions on a case before it gets to trial. But sometimes the solicitor has to wait three months to get a ten-minute appointment with a Master.

Delays are not always against the plaintiff's interests. Sometimes it takes a long while for the full extent of the injury – and therefore the size of the claim – to become apparent. According to one former Chairman of the Bar, the process works fairly well:

> The pre-trial work is very important for the purpose of having the case properly prepared and fit for trial, and it necessarily takes some time. It's a process which is designed to enable the trial when it happens to produce the right answer. One could cut down on it, at the expense of having a more hit-and-miss process or trial. Inevitably there would be more cases in which crucial material was overlooked or wasn't available which might affect the outcome.
>
> For the perfect system of justice you would perhaps have even more extensive investigations than are now possible. One could, I suppose, cut down the length of time that the pre-trial work takes, but I think at the expense of the satisfactory nature of the outcome, in terms of the right answer for the right party to the litigation ... So far as delays in civil litigation are concerned, I think the balance is about right.

Lord Devlin (in *What's Wrong With the Law,* ed. Zander, BBC, 1970) concentrates on a more basic point, affecting both cost and time:

> Various committees have from time to time been appointed to investigate the cost of litigation and they have been able to prune expenditure here and there but

never to make any substantial impact. Nor will they so long as they do not dare to tackle the two features of our procedure which truly account for its enormous cost. These are the adversary system and the insistence upon oral evidence. Under the adversary system each side prepares its case in secret, giving away as little as possible to its opponent. In this way the work is trebled, each side conducting an investigation on its own and then the two meeting in confrontation. As for the insistence upon oral evidence, this not only produces a heavy bill for the attendance of witnesses but means, since the judge has to make a note of the evidence, that the pace of the trial proceeds at the speed at which he can write instead of at the speed at which he can read . . .

In my opinion we shall not make any worthwhile saving in the cost of litigation so long as we accept it as the inalienable right of every litigant to have the whole of his evidence and argument presented by word of mouth...

The fallacy inherent in our High Court procedure of civil litigation is . . . that where justice is concerned, time and money are no object. We think of British justice as an ideal into which such sordid considerations ought not to enter. We refuse to associate with it such homely maxims as that half a loaf is better than no bread. But is it right to cling to a system that offers perfection for the few and nothing at all for the many? Perhaps: if we could really be sure that our existing system was perfect. But of course it is not. We delude ourselves if we think that it always produces the right judgment. Every system contains a percentage of error; and if by slightly increasing the percentage of error, we can substantially reduce the percentage of cost, it is only the idealist who will revolt.

Fifteen years after Lord Devlin made those remarks, High Court injury cases still take four, five, six or more years from accident to conclusion. In the High Court, cases cost £50 or £70 on average for every £100 awarded in damages, depending on the basis of calculation; in the county court the costs add up to £125 or £175 for every £100 awarded. But the Civil Justice Review, appointed by the Lord Chancellor in 1985 to suggest reforms to reduce delay, cost and complexity, has come up with radical proposals which, if implemented, could make accident claims much speedier and cheaper.

These include taking smaller cases out of the trial system and instead having an adjudicator make a ruling after studying the papers.

For cases which stay in the trial system, much shorter and stricter time limits would be laid down, and both sides would have to lay their cards on the table much earlier and more fully than they do now. Judges would be provided with a written outline of the case and witnesses' statements in advance, witnesses' evidence would be given partly in writing and lawyers' speeches would be curtailed. And solicitors who handle personal injury litigation would need special qualifications.

Some commentators argue that compensation should be removed from the legal system altogether, at least for some types of injury.

Lord Denning, in *What Next in the Law* (Butterworths, 1982), had this to say:

> Our law as to personal injuries is entirely out of date. It evolved during the time when all civil actions were tried by juries and all damages were assessed by juries. It was formed in relation to horse transport and rail transport. It is quite inapplicable to transport by motor vehicles. These bring death and disablement on all sides. Many of those injured are unable to prove that the driver was negligent. It is imperative, as a matter of justice, that there should be introduced a system for compensation to victims even though they cannot prove negligence: no-fault liability as it is called.

He was supporting a recommendation of the Royal Commission on Civil Liability and Compensation for Personal Injury, chaired by Lord Pearson, which reported in 1978. The Commission proposed a radical reform which would lift most traffic accident victims out of the legal process altogether. No longer would compensation depend on pinning the blame on someone else. The new system would remove the element of chance which can give thousands of pounds to one road accident victim, while another, with equally severe injuries, gets nothing – simply because the first happened to be knocked down in front of reliable witnesses with good memories, while the second was hit on a lonely stretch of road.

Of the 400,000 people injured on the roads every year, only around one-quarter succeed in getting any money from the driver or his insurance company, according to a survey done for the Pearson Commission. The rest lose out for a variety of reasons: some don't even realize they have a claim, or don't know how to go about making one; others think the accident was their own fault or nobody's fault; some simply don't want to make a fuss. Of the claims that proceed, the more serious the injury, the longer it takes to get the money. Small claims are usually settled fairly quickly; big ones are more likely to go to court or be settled only at a late stage.

Apart from its unfairness, said the Pearson Commission, the

present system is expensive and inefficient. The cost of administration – legal fees, expenses in handling claims, and so on – comes to nearly as much each year as the total amount paid out in damages. They proposed a no-fault system of compensation for road accident victims, administered by the state and funded by a levy of perhaps one penny on a gallon of petrol, in effect putting the burden on those who do the damage. Anyone damaged by a vaccine should also be able to claim compensation from the state without proving fault, they said.

The Pearson Commission studied no-fault schemes operating in other countries, particularly New Zealand, where victims of all sorts of accidents – not just traffic accidents – are covered. But they rejected no-fault compensation for work accidents or medical mistakes. And they recommended that road accident victims should still have the right to sue, as they do at present, even after a no-fault scheme was introduced. This would allow anyone who suffered a big loss – because he was earning a particularly high income before the accident – or anyone with serious and lingering injuries, to get more than the state compensation scheme would give him.

The trouble with royal commissions is that they tend not to complete their deliberations within the lifespan of the government which appointed them. More often than not, by the time they report, the subject of their concern seems to have lost the urgency which prompted their setting up. Shelves in government offices groan under the weight of unimplemented royal commission reports, and Pearson seems to have joined their number: 'Scurvy treatment by an ungrateful government', as Lord Denning describes it.

So people like Anne Jones will have to continue to struggle through the legal process to get justice. And many less fortunate than Anne Jones will get no justice at all.

# CHAPTER VIII

# DIVORCE

Around 50,000 accident victims start legal proceedings every year. Chapter VII charts the progress of just one of them, Anne Jones, through the legal system and sees her emerge £31,000 better off. But for many more people – around 300,000 a year – the accident which embroils them in the legal process is the breakdown of their marriage. This chapter follows Mary James, one of the 300,000, through the divorce machine.

Mary James is thirty-one. She and her husband, Bill, have been married for ten years, and have two children – David, nine, and Paul, eight. Just over two years ago, Bill started going out with Jane, a girl at his office, and two months later he left Mary and moved in with Jane. Mary was devastated, but she kept hoping Bill would come to his senses and come back to her. He went on paying the mortgage and the household bills, very much as before. But gradually she has come to accept the fact that her marriage is over, and recently she has started seeing another man regularly, though she has no immediate intention of remarrying.

Now Bill is talking about selling the house, which he and Mary own jointly, and using his share to buy a new flat for himself and Jane. Mary is worried about her position, and decides to see a solicitor to find out what her rights are and to see about getting a divorce.

Divorce is part of the civil law. The process for sorting out disputes between divorcing spouses has a lot in common with an action for breach of contract or negligence. Usually each side is represented by a separate lawyer. Each puts forward his or her own side of the case. A judge or registrar decides the result mainly on the evidence that the two sides put before him.

But divorce sits uneasily as part of the judicial process. Decisions are based much more on welfare principles – such as the needs of the parties and the best interests of the children – and less on strict legal rights. Many judges and lawyers believe divorce should be removed from the ordinary courts and dealt with in special family courts, with more of a social welfare and less of a judicial emphasis, with husband and wife helped to reach their own agreements and the whole process conducted along more 'inquisitorial' – fact-finding – lines,

153

rather than the present 'adversarial' approach, which tends to foster conflict. As Stephen Cretney, Professor of Law at the University of Bristol, has put it: 'It may be argued that a system of accusatorial court hearings, almost inevitably institutionalizing the parties' hostility towards one another, is not well suited to the satisfactory resolution of family problems' (*Family Law*, Sweet and Maxwell, 3rd edn., 1979).

Though the Finer Committee on One-Parent Families strongly recommended family courts as far back as 1974, it was not until 1985 that an official working party was set up to look at possible models. And while the present system, which coped adequately with 25,000 divorces a year in the late fifties, struggles to deal with an annual toll of 150,000, family courts are unlikely to become a reality in the near future.

## Getting a Divorce

At present all divorces start in the county court. Not every county court hears divorces, but some courts are designated divorce county courts and deal with divorces along with their other business. In London, the Divorce Registry at Somerset House is the equivalent of a divorce county court.

Getting a divorce is now much simpler than it used to be. In the vast majority of cases you no longer have to go to court and answer embarrassing questions about the reasons your marriage broke down. The whole process is just a matter of getting the paperwork right. Now that getting the divorce decree is largely a rubber-stamping exercise not much more difficult than filling in a tax return, the court battles revolve around what happens after the divorce: who gets the children? How is the property divided? How much maintenance should be paid?

The process starts with a petition for divorce which is filed with the court. A husband and wife cannot jointly petition for a divorce; one or the other must start the ball rolling. No one can petition for divorce within the first year of marriage.

Mary has a part-time typing job in an estate agents' office which brings in about £65 a week, so she qualifies for advice and help with preparing her petition under the legal aid 'green form scheme' (see Chapter IX). In the James' case, since Mary is asking for the divorce, she is known as the 'petitioner'. Bill is called the 'respondent'. About 70 per cent of divorces are started by wives, but exactly the same rules apply if the husband is petitioning for divorce.

Although official policy is firmly in favour of allowing dead marriages to be decently buried, divorce is still not available on demand. Grounds still have to be proved. Since 1971, the law says the only ground is that the marriage has 'irretrievably broken down'. The evidence of the breakdown is provided by proving one of five 'facts' (which, confusingly, many lawyers still refer to as 'grounds').

Mary's solicitor tells her that her petition will have to be based on one of the following:

Fact A: that her husband has committed adultery and she finds it intolerable to live with him.

Fact B: that her husband has behaved in such a way that she cannot reasonably be expected to live with him.

Fact C: that her husband has deserted her for a period of at least two years.

Fact D: that she and her husband have lived apart for at least two years, and he consents to the divorce.

Fact E: that she and her husband have lived apart for at least five years (in this case, his consent is not necessary).

Theoretically, the concept of the 'guilty' party and the 'innocent' party has gone from divorce. When divorce by consent was introduced, there were great hopes that it would lead to more civilized divorces, but the hopes were unfounded. Adultery and 'unreasonable behaviour' are still the most popular reasons for divorce, accounting for 30 per cent and 38 per cent of divorces granted in 1984, with divorce by consent trailing in third place. It is no coincidence that the two most used facts are the only ones which allow a quick divorce; the others all mean a wait of at least two years. Nearly 90 per cent of the unreasonable behaviour petitions are brought by wives, presumably wanting a quick divorce so that their financial claims can be sorted out without delay.

Some divorce lawyers think that the existence of the unreasonable behaviour fact is partly to blame for the knock-down, drag-out battles which some divorces become – often at great expense to the public purse, since many are conducted with the help of legal aid. Airing the dirty laundry of a rocky relationship – particularly when incidents in which both sides may have been at fault are given a one-sided slant – is hardly likely to put the spouse on the receiving end into a reasonable frame of mind. As the Law Society points out in its paper, 'A Better Way Out' (1979):

> Even though the 'accused' may not want to oppose divorce proceedings, indeed may welcome them, resentment at having to accept the blame for a situation for which he or she may feel the other spouse to be as much or more responsible can provoke quarrels where none need have occurred, and lead to bitter disputes about matters which would otherwise have seemed of little consequence.

Many lawyers believe that divorce should no longer be based on fault at all. The Law Society has recommended a change to a single ground for divorce: irretrievable breakdown shown by just one year's separation. The subject is currently under study by the Law Commission.

Mary decides to base her petition on two years' separation with Bill's consent. She has already discussed the question of divorce with Bill, and he says he won't object. A 'statement of arrangements' for the children will be sent to the court with the petition and the James' marriage certificate. This gives the court details of the children's accommodation, schooling, financial support, and arrangements for them to see their father.

The court sends Bill a copy of the divorce papers, which he acknowledges, confirming that he consents. Even where a divorce is not based on consent, in most cases the respondent will not raise any objections to the divorce. Many respondents whose first reaction is to 'defend' the divorce, to deny that the marriage has broken down or to object to the allegations made against them, are advised against it by their solicitors. Defending a divorce is usually a fruitless and expensive exercise, because most judges take the view that a marriage has irretrievably broken down if one party is determined to end it, irrespective of the feelings of the other partner in the marriage. Though legal aid is theoretically available, it is difficult to get for defending a divorce. Well over 99 per cent of divorces are undefended, like the James'.

The court sends Mary's solicitor a copy of Bill's acknowledgement. This is her cue to move on to the next stage, completing a sworn document called an 'affidavit of evidence' confirming that the contents of the petition are true and that there are grounds for the divorce. Now that petitioners no longer have to appear in court, this takes the place of the oral evidence which used to be required.

At this stage, the registrar of the court will look at the papers and see that everything is in order, and that the case for the divorce has been made out. Registrars are senior judicial officers, who are not judges, but who make many of the decisions in the county court. In divorce cases some decisions are made by registrars and some by judges. Registrars rule in disputes about property and money; judges decide who should have custody of the children.

If the registrar is satisfied with the petition he will certify that the divorce should be granted. The date is fixed for the judge to pronounce the divorce decree in open court. A list of names of couples to be divorced is read out and the judge simply states that each of them is granted a 'decree nisi'. There is no need for any of the couples to attend court. The decree nisi is only a provisional decree. The marriage is not finally ended until the decree is made absolute, usually six weeks later. Only after decree absolute has been pronounced are the parties free to marry again.

Before the decree can be made absolute the court will have to be satisfied about the arrangements made for the care of the children. Mary's proposals were set out in the 'statement of arrangements' filed with the petition: she proposes that the children should continue to live with her, going to their present schools, and that they continue to see Bill regularly. (Mary and Bill have agreed to be flexible about Bill's access to the children, rather than stick to a strict formula, say, once a fortnight.) An appointment is made, often for the same day as the decree nisi is pronounced, for the petitioner (and the respondent if he wishes) to see the judge in his private rooms. The judge will ask some questions about the arrangements and will want to know if anything has changed since the original proposals. In most cases the judge will approve the arrangements. If he is not entirely satisfied, he may ask for further information, or he may delay deciding until some outstanding difficulty has been resolved – for example, over housing. Or he may ask a court welfare officer to investigate the situation and make a report. He can, in unusual circumstances, allow the decree to be made absolute in spite of the fact that he is not satisfied with the arrangements for the children, but this is rare. Bill and Mary have agreed that Mary should have custody, and the judge makes a custody order then and there, and an order for Bill to have 'reasonable access' to the children. Critics of the present procedure point out that once a judge pronounces himself satisfied, there is nothing to prevent the parents changing the arrangements the next day, and the court would be none the wiser.

## Reaching Agreement

Once the decree nisi is pronounced, or at any time after, the long-term financial arrangements can be sorted out. In many cases, a divorcing couple will decide these matters for themselves by negotiation rather than fight it out in court. Solicitors for the husband and wife may have been negotiating the terms of the divorce settlement for some time – and may possibly have reached agreement – before the divorce petition is even filed. The petition itself may even have been a bargaining counter in the negotiations. A wife who knows her husband wants to remarry quickly but has no grounds on which to divorce her may hold out for more money in return for agreeing to divorce him on the grounds of his adultery. Divorce has its elements of gamesmanship, just as much as any other branch of civil litigation.

Divorce gives the parties the right to make certain claims on each other and on the family assets. Both husband and wife have equal right to claim, but in practice claims are usually made by the wife, since she usually owns and earns less. A wife can ask, for example, for regular maintenance payments for herself and the children, a share of the family home or the right to live in it, or a lump sum.

Legal aid is available to bring – or contest – any of these claims, as long as the financial criteria are met. Divorce is one of the biggest drains on the civil legal aid budget, eating up two-thirds of the total spent every year.

Bill and Mary have managed to agree on their divorce and the custody of the children. Bill has no objections to paying for the children's support, plus a small amount for Mary. The main sticking point is the house. Mary's solicitor applies for a legal aid certificate to cover the cost of negotiating with Bill's solicitor and, if necessary, going to court.

In the event, agreement is reached without too much difficulty. Bill's solicitor persuades him that a court would be unlikely to order the house to be sold as long as the children needed a home. Mary's main concern is to have a secure home for herself and the children. So she agrees to forgo any maintenance for herself if Bill transfers the family home to her. She will take a full-time job and pay the mortgage out of her earnings. Bill will continue to pay £70 a month for each of the two boys. The court is asked to approve the agreement and it is made into a court order.

Just as many claims in other areas of the civil law (like personal injuries) are settled out of court because the person liable knows he has to pay in any event and wants to avoid having to pay all the costs of an expensive trial as well, so many financial claims on divorce are settled by negotiation.

How is agreement reached? There are guidelines, based on what a court would order, just as there are guidelines for damages in accident cases. In divorce the sums are harder to do because of the court's wide discretion and all the factors that have to be weighed up: the length of the marriage, the contributions of the parties, whether there are children, the needs and responsibilities of the husband and wife in the future, any disabilities, and so on. In most cases, little weight if any is given to the conduct of the parties.

Both husband and wife have to disclose their earnings and assets and their expenses. The object of the exercise is to reach a settlement tailor-made for the particular couple while saving the cost, uncertainty and possibly bitterness of a court application. For example, they may prefer a clean break, with a share-out of the family assets and no maintenance for the wife. The courts have been increasingly favouring this solution in recent years, and the 1984 Matrimonial and Family Proceedings Act emphasizes the desirability of self-sufficiency for both ex-spouses if possible. If the wife thinks she is likely to remarry, she may forgo any claims to maintenance – which ceases on remarriage – in favour of a lump sum, which she can keep even if she marries again.

When a settlement is reached, the couple can ask to have it made into a court order, just as if it had been decided by the court. A court order may be worded so as to bar either party from any further claims on the other. If an open-ended order is made for weekly or monthly maintenance, either spouse can come back to the court later to ask for it to be increased or decreased. But property, once transferred, can't be transferred back, and only one lump sum can be awarded.

## Fighting it out

If a couple can't agree on financial terms, then either spouse – husband or wife, petitioner or respondent – can make an application to the court. In practice, almost all applications are made by wives, although the law makes no distinction. Wives are rarely ordered to maintain their husbands, but they may be ordered to pay something towards the upkeep of children living with their father, and husbands have been awarded large lump sums in a few cases.

Many millions of pounds in legal aid are spent each year on wrangles between divorcing spouses over money, property and children. A legal aid certificate can be a powerful bargaining counter, particularly if held by only one party to the contest. Many more wives than husbands qualify for legal aid, and wives can use the threat of legal proceedings – with the risk that the husband may have to pay both his own and his wife's costs – to wangle a bigger share of the cake. A few bitter wives will refuse all reasonable offers, determined to put the spouse who has 'wronged' them to the maximum expense and inconvenience. On the other hand, some husbands see no reason why they should continue to pay for a wife they are no longer getting the benefit of, and will try to hide their assets or dispose of them, and thwart maintenance claims by refusing to work.

## Money and Property

Most divorce petitions include a 'prayer' asking for maintenance, property and so on – usually, in fact, asking for the whole range of possible orders. This is almost always thrown in even if the petitioner has no intention of making any claims at all, 'just in case'. The petitioner who fails to ask for an order in the petition has an extra step to go through if she later wants to pursue her claim: she will have to ask the court's permission to go ahead with her application. As long as the application is there on the record, a husband is never entirely safe from a claim by an ex-wife, even if he has heard nothing from her for years. And orders, once made, can be varied up or down, as the circumstances of either party change. For instance, if the husband takes on the responsibility of supporting a new family or the wife moves in with another man, the husband can apply to have the maintenance payments reduced. On the other hand, if the wife has to stop working because of illness, or the husband gets a big salary increase, she can apply for bigger payments. However the court can also rule that there should be a clean break and a wife's payments should stop, either immediately or after a period of time. The court can only award one lump sum, and whatever is decided about the family home will stand. There is no question of coming back years later and asking the court to change its mind, though if one party thinks the court has made a wrong order an appeal against it is possible within a reasonable time.

You won't be able to get a lump sum or share of property if you remarry before you make your application, but the usual step of including the application in the petition will save you from that pitfall. Remarrying before the court hears the application won't prevent you from getting something, but it might affect the amount.

Hearings are in private and nobody not connected with the case is allowed to attend. The registrar will need to have all the evidence before him at the hearing, in order to reach a decision. Both husband and wife will have to file affidavits with the court, setting out in full their capital, income and expenses. The registrar will want to have a complete financial picture of both spouses – not only at that time, but for the foreseeable future.

In making his decision, the registrar will weigh up all the factors, but the decision will come down to the amount of money and property available to be shared out, and the needs of the two ex-spouses and their children. There is a rough guideline – a holdover from the days when divorces were granted by the ecclesiastical courts, but enshrined in an important judgement by Lord Denning in 1973 – which says that, as a rough rule of thumb, the husband's and wife's incomes should be added together, and she should be given enough to bring her to one-third of the total. (If she already earns that much, she may be given a nominal sum, say 5p a year, which will allow her to come back for more at a later date if circumstances change.)

Later cases have emphasized that the so-called 'one-third rule' is only a very rough starting-point, useful only in middle-income cases, and the registrar should also take account of other factors – such as tax relief which is available on maintenance payments, large mortgage payments, the husband's second family and the fact that the wife may be able to claim supplementary benefit – and adjust the amount up or down accordingly. In one case the Court of Appeal reduced a maintenance order based on the one-third rule from £350 to £150 a month, because of these factors.

In deciding what a husband can afford to pay, the court looks at all the circumstances – including the fact that he has a second wife or live-in girlfriend. If Bill and Mary had fought over maintenance, the earnings of Bill's girlfriend, Jane, would have been weighed up in the scales. This is not done by any crude mathematical formula – the court will not, for example, just lump Bill's and Jane's incomes together. The fact that Jane is self-supporting and contributing to expenses simply means that Bill can pay more than he otherwise might. But the end result, many second wives argue, is that they are forced to work to keep their husbands' first wives.

Maintenance for children is usually geared to the actual cost of feeding and clothing them and providing for their other expenses, in line as far as possible with the family's standard of living.

In deciding what should happen to the family home, the main consideration is that both parties should have a roof, and particularly that the children should have a home. Because whoever has the children is usually allowed to stay in the home, fights ostensibly over custody of the children may actually be about the right to live in the family home.

The home will not often be transferred outright to one spouse, except possibly as a quid pro quo if she gives up her claims to maintenance, or if the court thinks the man won't pay regularly. What happens more often is that the court awards a proportion of the property's value to the husband and a proportion to the wife: half and half, or one-third/two-thirds, for example. The wife, if she has children, may be allowed to live in the house until the children are seventeen, or finish their education, after which the house will be sold and the proceeds divided. If this solution would be likely to leave the wife in her middle age without enough to buy another house, the court may decide to let her stay in the house for life, or until she remarries, possibly paying the husband a small rent for the use of his share. If the couple are young and childless, the house may be sold and the money split. Or one spouse may be ordered to raise a lump sum to buy the other out. The court has a wide discretion. The legal ownership of the home counts for little. The fact that one of the spouses has a secure home provided by a new partner is much more relevant.

## The Children

Decisions about children are made in a separate hearing. Most parents manage to agree on custody, and fewer than one in ten divorces involves a custody fight in court. Access to the children by the absent parent is a much more fruitful battleground. Some cases go on for years, with endless court applications and arguments over access, running up thousands of pounds in bills in the process. The overriding factor the court will look to in reaching any decision about children is: what is in the child's best interests? Judges usually rely on the reports of court welfare officers, who visit both parents in their homes, often talk to the children and visit their schools, and make recommendations to the court.

Access is clearly an emotional problem rather than a legal one, and the law offers no effective remedy to the father whose ex-wife denies him access. Theoretically, a mother who refuses to comply with an access order can be sent to prison for contempt of court. But what judge would be willing to send her?

Conciliation is a new development which has taken some of the sting out of clashes over children of divorce. Conciliation services have been set up around the country to help divorcing parents resolve their grievances instead of perpetuating them through fights over their children, and some courts bring warring spouses together with a divorce court welfare officer to see if they can be helped to work out their own custody and access agreements.

## The Future

In England and Wales, court procedure for dealing with families is a hotch-potch. Three different courts are involved – the High Court, the county court and the magistrates' court – all overlapping each other, but operating by different rules. Divorce is not available in the magistrates' court, but people who are separated but not yet divorced can apply to the magistrates' court for maintenance and custody orders. A unified family court, now under consideration, could end the confusion and make divorce less of a battleground.

Changes in divorce procedure to make the process simpler and less acrimonious are likely following recommendations by an official committee under Dame Margaret Booth, a High Court judge. Instead of the present procedure, where one spouse brings divorce proceedings against the other, couples may be able to petition jointly for divorce. And petitions based on unreasonable behaviour may no longer recite the respondent's matrimonial failings in neatly lettered paragraphs. Rather than a succession of time-wasting hearings on custody, access, maintenance, division of property and the right to occupy the family home – all of which may be dealt with separately under the existing system – the Booth Committee suggested an initial hearing at which the court would grant the divorce decree, make orders about matters on which the parties agreed, define the issues still in dispute, and allow conciliation on those issues. The Committee's proposals, if accepted, would mean more couples resolving their own post-divorce squabbles, rather than having solutions imposed on them by the courts.

# CHAPTER IX

# THE PRICE OF JUSTICE

The solicitor was explaining his charges to a new client. 'My charging rate is £50 an hour,' he said. The client leapt up and bolted for the door, pausing only to call over his shoulder: 'I would have said goodbye, only I can't afford to.'

Fear of the cost is one of the most powerful deterrents to using lawyers' services. Even if a client overcomes his initial fear and gets across the threshold of a solicitor's office, he worries about how the costs are mounting up, as the invisible taxi meter ticks away. Are clients' anxieties about costs justified? Do solicitors overcharge, and are there any controls on their charges? The Royal Commission on Legal Services looked at the whole question of lawyers' fees, and came to the conclusion that they were not too high for the work done. But they thought that the legal processes themselves – particularly in conveyancing and litigation – should be simplified, with a view to reducing delay and cost.

## LAWYERS' CHARGES

For a solicitor, time is money. In most firms, every solicitor, legal executive and articled clerk has an hourly expense rate, based on his share of the firm's expenses, including his salary (or a notional salary if he is a partner). The expense rate represents the actual cost to the firm of doing the work, not including any profit. A typical medium-sized firm outside London might have expense rates of about £18 an hour for articled clerks, £25 an hour for legal executives and assistant solicitors, and £35 an hour for partners. But the hourly rate the solicitor actually charges his client – his 'charging rate' – will include a profit element as well.

Because the rates are related to the firm's expenses, firms with lower overheads can charge less than practices paying high rents, rates and salaries. Overheads in the average practice eat up about two-thirds of the fees earned. A solicitor practising from his home with his wife as secretary will be able to charge considerably lower rates than a large firm renting expensive city-centre offices and paying high salaries. And a firm in central London will charge more than a practice in a small market town in Lincolnshire. For most types of work, a partner in an outer London practice will probably charge somewhere in the region of £45 to £60 an hour.

The size of the bill which eventually lands on the client's doormat may depend not only on the time spent on the job, but also on such factors as the skill and knowledge and effort involved, the value of any property dealt with, and the importance of the matter to the client. A transaction which involves a great deal of money may justify a higher fee than one where less money is at risk, but which takes the same length of time.

For a run-of-the-mill house conveyancing job, a solicitor with an expense rate of £35 an hour taking six hours to do the job could justify charging:

| | |
|---|---|
| ½ per cent of the house price (£60,000) ......... | £300 |
| Plus 5 hours x £35 .......................... | £175 |
| Total fee | £475 |

But with fierce competition between solicitors for conveyancing, some will do the job for less – say, ½ per cent plus £100 or ½ per cent plus £50. A few charge a flat fee for conveyancing. If you ask, many solicitors will give you a written estimate of their charges for conveyancing and the other costs such as stamp duty and search fees.

## Court proceedings

In cases where court proceedings may be necessary – claiming damages for an accident, for example – no solicitor will commit himself to a firm price in advance, because the way in which a case will progress is to a large extent out of his control. So much depends on how easy or difficult it is to persuade the other side to pay up. A few letters back and forth may be sufficient. Or the case may go to a full trial, or a settlement may only happen at the door of the court.

For this sort of work, and for divorce and defending criminal charges – unless the client has legal aid – most solicitors will ask for a down payment at the beginning of the case, a sum 'on account of costs', as they call it. This could be around £250 for a county court action, £700 for a High Court case. But it could be more or less, depending on the type of case. As the case progresses, most solicitors deliver interim bills – showing how the money in hand has been spent – and ask for further sums on account. A client who is convicted, or who loses his case or abandons it, is not likely to regard his solicitor's bill as a matter of high priority, so the prudent solicitor likes to cover most of his costs as he goes along. This practice also keeps the client from running up an enormous bill without his knowledge. If he prefers, a client can authorize the solicitor to incur costs only up to a certain amount – say, £200. When the limit is reached, the solicitor will have to seek his approval before doing any more work. Alternatively the client can ask for an account every month, showing where he stands.

Costs include solicitors' fees, 'disbursements' – out-of-pocket expenses such as court fees, payments to doctors and other expert witnesses, barristers' fees – and VAT. A medical specialist will charge in the region of £50 for a written report, and £250 or more for a day's attendance at court. A consultant engineer, who may be asked for an opinion on how a road accident happened, is likely to charge in the region of £175 to £200 per day.

Barristers' fees are more variable than solicitors' charges. Though top specialists can command high rates for advisory work, fees for pre-trial paperwork are on the whole not high. For example, the court guidelines for accident cases allow £28 to £38 for drafting the statement of claim (the victim's statement of his case and the compensation he hopes to get) and £38 for giving an opinion on how much an injury is worth. The fees for trial work, however, make up for the underpayment on the paperwork. In the more difficult case, using a QC, the client is paying for the constant attendance of three lawyers – the QC, his junior, and the solicitor or his representative.

If a case goes to court, barristers are entitled to a 'brief fee', to cover preparation plus the first day of the trial, and a daily sum, called a 'refresher'. A QC in a High Court accident case can usually expect a minimum brief fee of £750 plus refreshers of £350 a day, a junior around half as much. Not surprisingly, fewer than 1 per cent of personal injury cases reach court. One side's costs for five days in court on a contested personal injury case, with a QC, can run to around £10,000 including the solicitors' preparation.

Many brief fees are much less, some much higher. A raw barrister handling a guilty plea in the magistrates' court will count himself lucky to get £50, while top commercial silks can command brief fees in the tens of thousands for complicated cases.

Pressures to settle out of court are strong. A trial can easily double the costs on both sides. But our legal system puts an extra hazard in the litigant's path: the danger that he might end up paying both sides' costs. In litigation the usual rule is that the loser pays the winner's costs as well as his own. Where cases are settled out of court, the party who pays up usually agrees to pay his opponent's costs as well. Even the winner may not get off scot free, however. In many cases, the winner will have to pay part of his own solicitor's fees. This is because the court – the ultimate arbiter of costs – allows costs to be charged on different scales according to who is to pay.

A solicitor is entitled to be paid all costs incurred by him on his client's behalf which the client has authorized. When assessing the costs to be paid by the losing party, the court may disallow some of these costs and the client will have to make up the difference.

In legal aid cases, the shortfall, if any, will be met from any contributions the legally-aided person has made towards the cost of his case.

## Challenging a bill

Except in small cases, bills to be paid by the legal aid fund are always scrutinized by the court to see if every item is reasonable. Confusingly, this process is called 'taxation', although it has nothing to do with the Inland Revenue. The winner's solicitor's bill, payable by the loser, may be 'taxed' in this way, or (more usually) the amount will just be agreed, if the loser's solicitor thinks it looks reasonable. Agreeing the bill saves a three or four month delay and the payment of a substantial fee (5 per cent of the bill) to the court.

A client dissatisfied with his own solicitor's bill can also have it taxed by the court, though few clients do. The bill need not be for court work: it could be for conveyancing or any other legal work. If the bill is reduced by one-fifth or more, the solicitor will have to pay the court taxing fee (5 per cent of the total bill). If not, the client has to pay. A far better way of challenging the fairness of a solicitor's bill – because there is no risk that the client will end up paying more – is to ask the solicitor to apply to the Law Society for a 'remuneration certificate'. This procedure is available for conveyancing, probate, commercial work, leases, tax advice, and most other types of legal work. But it cannot be used if the work involves court proceedings: for example, defending someone against a criminal charge, petitioning for divorce, applying for custody of a child or for maintenance, suing someone or being sued. In these cases taxation by the court is the only resort.

All the client has to do is ask the solicitor to set the wheels in motion. If he refuses, he can be reported for a breach of professional conduct. Filling in the application and sending his file off to the Law Society puts the solicitor to a lot of trouble, so he may knock a bit off the bill to save himself the time and effort. The Law Society looks at all the files, sees what work has been done, decides whether the charges are reasonable, and issues a certificate either upholding the charge or reducing it to a fair level. The review is free to the client and there is no chance of having the bill increased rather than reduced.

The Law Society is mainly concerned with whether the work done justifies the fees, but a solicitor who does an unnecessary amount of work on what should have been a straightforward job will find his fees marked down. And one who does a really shoddy job won't get the rate for a good job: in extreme cases he might get nothing at all.

In the High Court case described in Chapter VII this is what John Smith's insurance company would have had to pay towards Anne Jones' costs:

| | | |
|---|---:|---:|
| Solicitor's fees | £1,100.00 | |
| VAT | 165.00 | |
| | | £1,265.00 |
| Counsel's fees: | | |
| Statement of claim | 28.00 | |
| Advice on evidence | 45.00 | |
| Conference on payment-in | 38.00 | |
| Brief fee | 400.00 | |
| Total | 511.00 | |
| VAT | 76.65 | 587.65 |
| Doctor's fees: | | |
| Two reports | 120.00 | |
| Half-day's attendance at trial | 150.00 | |
| | | 270.00 |
| Police report | | 24.00 |
| Court fees: | | |
| Fee on writ | 60.00 | |
| Fee on setting case down for trial | 30.00 | 90.00 |
| TOTAL | | £2,236.65 |

Anne Jones' solicitor, Mr Long, estimates that if she had been a private client, not on legal aid, she would have had to pay (in addition to the costs paid by the insurance company):

| | |
|---|---:|
| Extra solicitor's charges | £210.00 |
| VAT | 31.50 |
| TOTAL | £241.50 |

See p.165 for an explanation of the reason the loser may not have to pay the winner's full costs.

## THE MIDDLE-INCOME TRAP

The result of litigation is uncertain and the individual is often faced with big guns, such as insurance companies, on the other side. If the evidence in an accident case is not clear-cut, insurance companies will sometimes deny liability and use delaying tactics, hoping the victim will lose heart, exhaust his funds and drop the case.

In cases where negligence is obvious, where the victim is bound to get some money, a recent court rule allows him to ask for some of his compensation to be paid early on, as soon as a writ has been issued. This interim award is particularly helpful for accident victims who don't qualify for legal aid, because they can use the payment to fund the litigation. In general, however, being outside the financial limits for legal aid in civil cases can be a disaster. Middle income families suffer most – they are too well-off to get legal aid, but not nearly rich enough to be able to afford major litigation.

Some of the greatest injustices occur when one party has been given legal aid, but the other has to pay for himself. A plaintiff with a legal aid certificate holds a trump card, and insurance companies on the other side will sometimes make a small 'nuisance value' settlement in a weakish case, just to avoid the costs of fighting it. This sort of expense is all part of an insurance company's overheads, paid for by its income from premiums. But an individual without legal aid who comes up against a legally-aided opponent is fighting an unequal battle. Large sums of legal aid money go to finance ex-wives' claims for maintenance and property in divorce cases. Husbands, often not much outside the legal aid limits themselves, paying their own costs and at risk of having to pay their wives' costs as well, hardly come on equal terms to the bargaining table.

Wives can suffer too, if they happen to have some small savings, which take them outside the legal aid net. In one divorce case the husband's income was just within the legal aid limits. The wife had little income, but her savings disqualified her from legal aid. As well as her own costs of over £3,000, she was ordered to pay her husband's costs of £6,000.

For someone without legal aid, fighting a legally-aided opponent in court is a case of 'heads you win, tails I lose', as the playwright William Douglas-Home found out recently. If the person on legal aid wins, you still have to pay his costs. If you win, he is unlikely to be ordered to pay much – if anything – towards your costs. The legal aid fund may pay them, but only if the court decides you would suffer 'severe financial hardship' in paying them yourself. And only defendants have any chance of getting their costs paid. A plaintiff suing a legally-aided defendant cannot even apply.

William Douglas-Home found himself sued for breach of copyright over one of his plays. He fought the claim and won. His opponent's costs were paid for by legal aid. But he was left to find his own costs, estimated, according to press reports, at £35,000.

In the High Court or county court, someone in his position will have his costs paid by legal aid only if the court decided he would otherwise suffer severe financial hardship. If a case goes to appeal, to the Court of Appeal of the House of Lords, a winner without legal aid is more likely to get his costs paid, because a different test is applied. The court only has to decide whether it would be 'just and equitable' for the legal aid fund to pay the costs. There is no mention of severe financial hardship. But the costs of appeals are higher and the risks greater. Very few individuals who are not legally aided get involved in appeals to the Court of Appeal or the House of Lords. Middle-income litigants rarely feature in their case reports. The ironic result is that, while individuals who win High Court cases against legally-aided opponents are often left to find their own costs, in the appeal courts a London borough has won its costs from the legal aid fund, and two huge multi-million-pound companies (Shell and BP) were awarded a reputed £33,000 in costs, courtesy of the taxpayer.

## LEGAL AID

Legal aid, introduced in 1950, was conceived as the second prong of the welfare state, the legal equivalent of the National Health Service, created two years earlier. A fund was set up, controlled by the Lord Chancellor, to pay lawyers in private practice to undertake litigation for the less well-off section of the population, along with their privately paid work. The work is done in just the same way, but in the end the costs are paid by the government, rather than the client, but on a slightly lower scale. In 1972 a separate Legal Advice and Assistance Scheme (the 'green form scheme') was set up to cover advice and help short of court proceedings, though it has now been extended to pay for a solicitor's representation in most civil cases in the magistrates' courts and before mental health review tribunals. The older scheme, known simply as civil legal aid, foots the bill for most types of cases in the county court, High Court, and appeal courts. Fights between ex-spouses over money, property and children, and accident cases, are the two biggest categories, but civil legal aid covers any dispute involving a civil court except libel and slander actions.

### The green form scheme

Virtually any sort of legal problem can be tackled under the green form scheme, and assistance can include such things as drafting a will, preparing a divorce petition, writing letters to landlords or troublesome neighbours or shopkeepers, or preparing a case for an industrial tribunal (but not representation at the tribunal). You qualify for green form help if your 'disposable capital' does not exceed £800 (£3,000 if the solicitor is representing you before a court or tribunal) and your 'disposable income' is not more than £114 a week. Capital includes savings, cash, building society accounts, bank accounts, investments, any valuable belongings such as furs and jewellery, but not your home or its contents. If you have dependants, you can subtract £200 for the first, £120 for the second, and £60 for every other dependant. The final figure is your disposable capital. Disposable income is gross weekly income less tax, national insurance, and an allowance for a spouse and for each dependant. For anyone on supplementary benefit or family income supplement or a disposable income of less than £54 a week, legal advice and assistance is completely free. Between £54 and £114 a week, you will get help, but will have to pay something towards it.

## Civil legal aid

To get legal aid for civil court proceedings – for example, to sue someone or to apply for maintenance or a share of property on divorce – you will have to pass two tests, a legal test and a financial test. The legal aid area office decides whether there is a good reason for bringing (or defending) the court action. The means test is more generous than for the green form scheme: a couple earning as much as £13,000 a year with three or four children and a big mortgage are likely to qualify for legal aid.

Disposable capital – worked out in the same way as for the green form scheme except that there are no allowances for dependants – normally must not exceed £4,710, (though an occasional exception is made where the costs of the case are likely to be very high). Anyone with capital below £4,710 but above £3,000, can expect to pay the excess over £3,000 towards the cost of the case. There is also an income hurdle to get over. Nobody with a disposable income of over £5,415 a year qualifies for legal aid. For civil legal aid, disposable income means gross yearly income less tax, national insurance, union dues, pension contributions, employment expenses, rent or mortgage payments, rates, water rates and allowances for a spouse and dependants. If the result is £2,255 or less, legal aid is free. If it is between £2,255 and £5,415 a contribution (usually a quarter of the excess over £2,255) has to be paid, in instalments.

One problem: for both the green form scheme and civil legal aid, a husband's and wife's income and capital are added together, even though only one of them may be going to court or taking legal advice – unless they happen to be fighting each other (as in divorce) or living apart. This rule partly explains why so much legal aid money goes on divorce. More divorced and separated people qualify for legal aid because only one income (and one nest-egg) is counted.

## The clawback

Legal aid has been a godsend for accident victims who might otherwise never have been able to get compensation for their injuries. But because of the way the legal aid scheme works, the result can be less happy when the fight is between a divorcing couple – or an unmarried couple splitting up – with the prize their home or savings.

Legal aid is not just a free gift. The fund's duty to the taxpayer is to get back as much as possible of the money it pays out, within the rules. So if somebody with legal aid wins a case against a company or individual without legal aid, any costs which the loser has to pay go straight into the legal aid fund. To these are added any contributions the winner has paid towards his legal aid. If the total is less than the fund has to pay out to the winner's lawyers, the balance is deducted from the legally-aided person's winnings. The clawback applies not only to property which a legally-aided person wins, but also to property which he manages to keep in the face of a court claim by somebody else.

The problem is not so acute where only the winner is legally-aided, because most of the costs will be paid by the loser. But suppose a husband and wife are both on legal aid, neither paying a contribution, and fighting over their one asset, the family home. Whoever wins, the legal aid fund will have nowhere to look for payment but to that home. The fund will take a sort of mortgage over it – called the 'statutory charge' – for the amount of the winner's legal costs, not only of the battle over the house but of any other disputes over the divorce, including children and maintenance. The mortgage will not be called in as long as the house remains the legally-aided person's home. But if it is sold, he or she can keep only the first £2,500 of whatever sum is realized. Anything over that – up to the full amount of the costs – goes to the legal aid fund. The balance, if there is any, goes to the legally-aided person.

Until quite recently, the money always had to be paid off as soon as the house was sold. But Mary Hanlon, a divorced mother of four, decided to challenge the rule. She wanted to sell her £25,000 house and buy a smaller one, but paying off the £8,000 bill for her six-year divorce battle would have left her with too little to buy a replacement. Her case, which went all the way to the House of Lords in 1980, decided that the Law Society, which runs the legal aid scheme, has a discretion to transfer the charge to a new house, rather than insisting on payment when the old house is sold. The discretion will not be exercised in every case. The Law Society has laid down guidelines for deciding whether it will allow the charge to be transferred to a new house. If the case falls outside the guidelines, the Law Society will expect to collect its money when the house is sold.

In a 1982 case an unmarried couple, both on legal aid, took their battle over their jointly owned home to the Court of Appeal. He was ordered to pay her £6,000 for her share. If a legally-aided person wins cash instead of a home, the legal aid fund takes its cut immediately. Since this case did not fall within one of the categories of cases which exempt the first £2,500, the bulk of her £6,000 disappeared 'into the maw of the legal aid fund', as one of the Court of Appeal judges put it. In 1984-5 the legal aid fund recouped over £12,000,000 through the operation of the statutory charge.

The charge is designed to put the legally-aided litigant in the same position as one who has to fund himself, and to act as an incentive to out-of-court settlements. Yet the Law Society admits in its legal aid handbook: 'The Law Society's statutory duty to recoup expenses by way of a charge on money or property recovered or preserved in the proceedings is one of the least understood conditions of legal aid.' Though both the legal aid form which every applicant signs and the applicant's leaflet include a note about the statutory charge, and the Law Society warns solicitors to explain it personally, many recipients of legal aid fail to grasp its full significance.

## Beyond legal aid

Few litigants enter the law machine without exposing themselves to substantial financial risks. Even those who are lucky enough to get legal aid can end up out of pocket. Is there a better way?

The Americans have a method of paying their lawyers which allows them to litigate without the fear of substantial loss. Lawyers can take on a case on a 'no win, no fee' basis. If they win, they get a percentage of the damages, usually around a third, but up to a half for more dodgy cases. If they lose, they get nothing. Levels of damages decided by juries in the USA are much higher than in England, where judges are responsible for fixing awards. American juries sometimes make awards of millions of dollars. So the winner is still left with a respectable sum, even after the lawyer's rake-off. This system of payment by contingency fees is forbidden to English lawyers. Both branches of the English legal profession are against it and the Royal Commission on Legal Services firmly rejected the idea.

Contingency fees work better in the American system, where each party to litigation bears his own costs. They cannot achieve the purpose of eliminating financial risk as long as the indemnity rule in English trials – that the loser pays the winner's costs – stays. The indemnity rule could be abolished, but it seems unfair that someone who is forced to take court action to get compensation should have his damages reduced by the cost of forcing the person at fault to pay up.

An alternative more suited to our legal system – to minimize the financial risks for middle-income litigants outside the scope of legal aid – has been suggested by the reform body, Justice: the idea of a 'contingency legal aid fund'. Only plaintiffs would be able to join, on payment of a registration fee. Winning plaintiffs would contribute a share of their damages, and the money would go to pay the costs of losing plaintiffs and their successful opponents. The Senate of the Inns of Court and the Bar have proposed a similar scheme. The Royal Commission on Legal Services, however, were unconvinced. Only plaintiffs with weak cases would want to join the scheme, they thought, so the fund would quickly run out of money. They also felt it was wrong that successful litigants should subsidize the unsuccessful, and that the heaviest levy should fall on the most seriously injured. The worse the injury, they pointed out, the bigger the damages, and the bigger the payment into the fund.

## Legal expenses insurance

Why shouldn't you be able to insure against the costs of involvement in legal proceedings, just as you can cover yourself against sickness or accidental injury or damage to your property? The West Germans, with no access to legal aid, have been insuring themselves against legal expenses for years. Legal expenses insurance came to Britain only twelve years ago, but the Royal Commission gave it the seal of approval and several companies now offer this cover, in many cases as an add-on to household and motoring policies.

Policies issued by the leading company in the field, DAS, generally exclude divorce and matrimonial disputes, wills, probate and succession, defamation (libel and slander) and planning applications. Legal Benefits Ltd offers a group policy at £100 a head, which pays conveyancing costs for home movers and divorce costs of up to £1,000 per couple, and includes an advisory service.

DAS policies cover the cost of defending criminal charges (other than those involving alleged dishonesty or deliberate violence), as well as suing or being sued, disputes over contracts of employment, and simple consumer claims. If an insured person loses, DAS pays his costs and the winner's costs up to the limit insured – normally £25,000. If he wins, the insurers pay the difference between his own solicitor's bill and the costs paid by the loser. In civil cases, the company will only give the go-ahead if there is a reasonable chance of success.

The Royal Commission on Legal Services agreed that legal expenses insurance filled a need, as long as many middle-income people could not get legal aid yet could not afford the high cost of going to law. But the Royal Commission's own suggestion for plugging the gap was one of the more radical proposals to come from a largely conservative report: abolish the means test for legal aid.

After all, the National Health Service is open to everyone. Having a cut-off point for legal aid was arbitrary, the Commission said. Someone just under the limit could enforce his rights, while his neighbour on £100 a year more would have to let his go by default. Even if all its recommendations for simplifying and speeding up the legal process were acted upon, the Commission argued, 'we are satisfied that the cost of any substantial piece of litigation will be formidable and beyond the pockets of nearly all private individuals'. The better off would have to pay a hefty contribution to the cost of their legal aid, but they would have the protection of knowing that their financial risk was limited. But with legal aid spending escalating, the chances of opening the scheme to everyone seem remote. Civil justice will continue to be the prerogative of the rich and the badly off, with those in the middle left out in the cold.

## Criminal legal aid

Survey after survey has shown that defendants who do not have a lawyer representing them at their trial are more likely to be convicted (sometimes wrongly) and, if convicted, to get a stiffer sentence than they would otherwise have got.

The lawyer knows his way around the procedure of the court, how best to present a case, what points to raise, what questions to ask. Quite often he can mean the difference between conviction and acquittal, because he sees a defence to the charge which would not occur to the layman.

Criminal legal aid is meant to ensure that, where the interests of justice demand it, a person charged with a criminal offence should have legal representation. To qualify for legal aid, a defendant has to show two things: first, that he cannot afford to pay for a lawyer himself, and second, that he *needs* a lawyer. The system does not assume that everyone charged with a criminal offence should have legal representation. It has to be in the interests of justice for him to have it. This is decided by the court, according to a set of criteria drawn up by a committee chaired by a former Lord Chief Justice, Lord Widgery.

These set out five circumstances in which legal aid should be granted. Some of the guidelines deal with special cases, such as language difficulties, or the fact that a complex point of law is involved or expert cross-examination is needed. But the most important rule says that legal aid should be granted whenever there is a serious risk that the defendant may lose his liberty, his job or his reputation.

Around 95 per cent of trials in the Crown Court, where the more serious charges are dealt with, are financed by legal aid. The costs of defending a serious charge are so high that very few defendants are able to meet them from their own pockets, and it is unquestionably in the interests of justice that someone charged with a serious crime – where the resources of the state are ranged against him – should have legal representation. In the magistrates' court, by contrast, many defendants are unrepresented. Some don't apply for legal aid: others do and are turned down.

The figures show that different magistrates' courts interpret the Widgery criteria in different ways. Courts have become much more consistent in recent years, however. Lord Gardiner, a former Lord Chancellor, described it as 'a public scandal' that in 1980 a defendant was eight times less likely to get legal aid at Highgate magistrates' court than at neighbouring Hampstead. In 1982, magistrates turned down around 20 per cent of legal aid applications. By 1984, however, the refusal rate had gone down to a nationwide average of 12 per cent, with the different legal aid areas varying between 10 per cent and 16 per cent. But disparities have not been completely ironed out: in 1984, while one east London court turned down 8 per cent of legal aid applicants, a neighbouring court refused 22 per cent. In the more serious cases, defendants turned down for legal aid can ask to have their applications reviewed by a criminal legal aid committee of the Law Society. Two out of three applications succeed.

Like civil legal aid, criminal legal aid by no means guarantees a free ride. Anyone with a disposable income of over £46 a week (see page 170 for the definition of 'disposable income') will be expected to contribute a weekly sum over a six-month period – £1 with income between £46 and £52, £2 between £52 and £56, and £1 for every £4 over £56 – together with any captial over £3,000.

Wives' and husbands' income and savings (and child benefit) are lumped together, just as for civil legal aid. Critics have pointed out that this can mean, in effect, wives paying out of their own earnings, savings, and child benefit to defend their husbands on criminal charges. But fears that the size of the contributions might lead defendants to refuse legal aid and appear in the dock without a lawyer – just as civil legal aid applicants often abandon their claims rather than pay a large contribution – have not been borne out.

At the end of the case, if the costs have worked out at less than the contributions paid, the difference is refunded. A defendant who is acquitted will usually get all his contributions back, unless the court thinks he brought the prosecution on himself.

# Afterword

The quality of English justice, according to the traditional formula, is the highest in the world, and the envy of other nations. Like many other expressions of national satisfaction, it contains a germ of truth, but begs a number of questions. Justice is not an absolute concept. It is complex and many-faced. It means different things to different people.

Comparing the English system with that of other countries is in any case an unrewarding exercise. It is easy to point to countries that have detention without trial and where there is government interference with the judiciary, and to take pride in our trial by jury and the integrity and independence of our own judges. But true comparisons are not with the totalitarian states, but with the democracies. Here, English justice is on less firm ground. It becomes more difficult to maintain certainty in the supremacy of our system. It is not that any one country can be pointed to as being superior. But there are many aspects of the legal machinery that function better, or more quickly or cheaper, elsewhere. In many other ways, however, our system does dispense justice of high quality. Whether English justice is the best depends on the problem it is faced with.

The last two decades have seen an enormous growth in the extent and variety of advice and financial help available to people with legal problems. The legal aid system and the proliferation of other avenues of advice – various organizations, ginger groups, local authorities and government departments, and numerous publications – have given millions of people the opportunity to participate in the legal process who previously would have been unable to pay the entrance fee.

As we have seen, however, increased access to the law machine is not always spread fairly, nor does it mean that justice is invariably attained once the individual has gained admission. The little man's passage through the legal process can seem like an obstacle course. From the moment an event gives rise to legal consequences, he is confronted by a succession of difficulties and possible injustices, some easier to overcome than others: the cost of going to law, unacceptable delays at various stages of the process, cumbersome procedures which militate against speedy and cheap justice, and a trial system which sometimes disguises rather than reveals the truth.

In addition, the individual is faced with a legal profession structured in a way that does not necessarily serve the best interests of the client, and with judges and magistrates who are chosen by a method which may not produce the best possible candidates.

Yet most people who get caught up in the law machine get some measure of justice, and on the whole the judiciary, the magistracy and the legal profession do a reasonable job. If there is disappointment with the system today, it is largely because expectations are so much higher than they have ever been. These are not conclusions capable of being quantified. There are no statistics of justice and injustice, even if it were possible to agree on the definition of those terms. One man's miscarriage of justice is another man's fair result. There are no absolutes. There are, as we have seen, many gaps and inequalities in the system. But most people would probably express general satisfaction after using it, and believe that they had had a fair deal, even if not the perfect result. Some – an unquantifiable minority – retain a justified grievance. For them, the boast that the English system of justice is the best in the world sounds hollow indeed.

# Index

# Index

## MORE ABOUT PENGUINS, PELICANS
## AND PUFFINS

For further information about books available from Penguins please write to Dept EP, Penguin Books Ltd, Harmondsworth, Middlesex UB7 0DA.

*In the U.S.A.*: For a complete list of books available from Penguins in the United States write to Dept DG, Penguin Books, 299 Murray Hill Parkway, East Rutherford, New Jersey 07073.

*In Canada*: For a complete list of books available from Penguins in Canada write to Penguin Books Canada Limited, 2801 John Street, Markham, Ontario L3R 1B4.

*In Australia*: For a complete list of books available from Penguins in Australia write to the Marketing Department, Penguin Books Australia Ltd, P.O. Box 257, Ringwood, Victoria 3134.

*In New Zealand*: For a complete list of books available from Penguins in New Zealand write to the Marketing Department, Penguin Books (N.Z.) Ltd, Private Bag, Takapuna, Auckland 9.

*In India*: For a complete list of books available from Penguins in India write to Penguin Overseas Ltd, 706 Eros Apartments, 56 Nehru Place, New Delhi 110019.

## THE CONSUMER, SOCIETY AND THE LAW

*Gordon Borrie and Aubrey L. Diamond*

This authoritative survey in which John Citizen, as customer and consumer, meets the law, covers all recent legislation and is thoroughly up-to-date.

We sign HP agreements, have furniture repaired, take clothes to the laundry, order food in restaurants, book holidays, open bank accounts, take out insurance policies, buy tickets to travel . . . but we seldom understand the law that covers the transaction until it is too late.

'This is the first volume of a new series . . . if the standard achieved in this first essay can be maintained the publisher will have done a better job to familiarize the general educated public with the elementary rules of law than any lawyer has achieved since Blackstone' – *Modern Law Review*

# THE WORKER AND THE LAW

*Third Edition    Lord Wedderburn*

This well-known book has been completely updated to provide a clear and comprehensive survey of contemporary labour law. The author, acknowledged the world over as an expert with extensive practical experience, offers the ideal guide to the three different structures established by Parliament for industrial relations since the 1960s. In addition, he shows how these are related to far wider and more important questions: the role of law in society, the controversies surrounding employment, the acute problems faced by legislators (and judges) in today's rapidly changing world.

'This book, written with great scholarship and with feeling, will be found of value and interest to the lawyer, the trade unionist, the employer and ordinary members of the public' – *New Society*

# THE PENGUIN GUIDE TO THE LAW

*John Pritchard*

Now firmly established as the guide to law for everyday use, this new, updated edition takes account of numerous changes in legislation – from ex-wives the maintenance of, to the abolition of solicitors' monopoly of conveyancing – and changes made by the courts.

'Tells you all you are likely to want to know – and probably more besides . . . A first-class reference book . . . thoroughly researched, clearly written and simply laid out, it is likely to justify the price many times over' – *The Times Educational Supplement*

'A quite remarkable volume which heralds a new approach to writing about the law and the legal profession specifically for the general public . . . Quite simply, it is the best lay person's book of, and about, the law' – *New Law Journal*

'A gem . . . The joy of the book is the clear, simple, but engaging style' – *Lawyer*